Anorexia Nervosa

The highly respected and widely known *Anorexia Nervosa: A Survival Guide for Sufferers and Friends* was written in 1997. This long-awaited new edition builds on the work of the first book, providing essential new and updated research outcomes on anorexia nervosa. It offers a unique insight and guidance into the recovery process for those who suffer from an eating disorder as well as advice and information for their loved ones. Written collaboratively by both an expert in the field and someone with personal experience of eating disorders, this book offers exceptional understanding of the issues surrounding the illness.

Divided into four sections, it includes:

- an outline of anorexia nervosa
- coping strategies for sufferers
- advice and information for families, carers and friends
- guidelines for professionals who are involved in the sufferer's life.

Families, friends, carers and professionals such as teachers and GPs are encouraged to read all sections in order to fully understand the illness. With an emphasis on collaboration and a layout that enables content to be referenced and read in any order, this book is an essential resource for anyone affected, directly or indirectly, by anorexia nervosa.

Janet Treasure, OBE, PhD, FRCP, FRCPsych, is Director of the Eating Disorder Unit at South London and Maudsley NHS Trust, and a Professor at Kings College, London.

June Alexander is an Australian writer and life writing educator who has a 40-year career in journalism and has battled eating disorders since the age of 11.

Anorexia Nervosa
A Recovery Guide for Sufferers,
Families and Friends

Second Edition

Janet Treasure and June Alexander

 Routledge
Taylor & Francis Group

LONDON AND NEW YORK

Second edition published 2013
by Routledge
27 Church Road, Hove, East Sussex BN3 2FA

Simultaneously published in the USA and Canada
by Routledge
711 Third Avenue, New York, NY 10017

Routledge is an imprint of the Taylor & Francis Group, an informa business

First edition published by Psychology Press 1997

British Library Cataloguing in Publication Data
A catalogue record for this book is available from the British Library

Library of Congress Cataloging in Publication Data
Treasure, Janet.
    Anorexia nervosa : a recovery guide for sufferers, families, and friends /
by June Alexander and Janet Treasure. — 2nd edition.
        pages cm
    Revised edition of Anorexia nervosa / Janet Treasure. 1997.
    1. Anorexia nervosa—Popular works.   2. Consumer education.
    I. Alexander, June, 1950–   II. Title.
    RC552.A5T74 2013
    616.85'262—dc23

                                                            2012044272

ISBN: 978-0-415-63366-6 (hbk)
ISBN: 978-0-415-63367-3 (pbk)
ISBN: 978-0-203-64019-7 (ebk)

Typeset in Times
by Keystroke, Station Road, Codsall, Wolverhampton

MIX
Paper from
responsible sources
FSC
www.fsc.org   FSC® C013056

Printed and bound in Great Britain by
TJ International Ltd, Padstow, Cornwall

Contents

About the authors

Janet Treasure

I have specialised in the treatment of eating disorders at the South London and Maudsley Hospital and King's College London for the majority of my career since 1981. I was trained by Gerald Russell when he was implementing the Maudsley approach to involving families in the treatment of anorexia nervosa.

My career has involved research targeting greater understanding of, and better treatments for, anorexia and bulimia. I have been able to translate some of the biological basics of the illness from genes and neuropsychology and scanning into treatment. This has been an iterative process as new questions and solutions are generated.

Much of my research focusing on the development of new treatments has been carried out collaboratively with, and often inspired by, patients and their families. This book is a sister to the book jointly written with Anna Crane and Grainne Smith, who have personal experience to share expertise and understanding with carers.

June Alexander

I developed anorexia nervosa at age 11 in 1962. Twenty years would pass before my illness was diagnosed. There were no wonderful books such as *Anorexia Nervosa: A Recovery Guide for Sufferers, Families and Friends* around when I was young. There was no wonderful researcher and clinician such as Professor Janet Treasure to reassure my parents or me that I had an illness and could recover.

I was in my thirties when my recovery journey began. But the eating disorder thoughts were deeply entrenched in my brain. I was also battling chronic anxiety and depression. I had no idea who I was. Untangling and separating the real me from the illness became a battle supreme. Although by now aware of the illness, I was afraid to let go of rules and thought processes on which I had survived, though barely functioned, since childhood. Losses were many.

There was, however, an ace card – my four young children. My love for them and a desire to watch them grow up, gave me the strength to gradually reach out – and let go. I began to trust therapists who, thanks to research outcomes, were becoming increasingly better informed. In my forties, I began to learn skills to recognise and defuse eating disorder thoughts. I progressively conquered fears, got in touch with suppressed feelings and rebuilt my identity. This involved learning to love, trust and respect myself, and eating three meals and three snacks every day, without fail. Easier said than done for someone with an eating disorder, but at age 55, I ticked all the boxes and crossed the line in regaining me. The years of struggle and hard work, tears and desperation, were over. My story is told in the memoir *A Girl Called Tim* and on my website www.junealexander.com.

At the time of writing, my life is filled with purpose. Writing books to give hope to others helps to turn my eating disorder experience into a big plus. I love life. I love every second. A loving partner, our children and grandchildren complete my happiness. They are my present and my future.

Early intervention with family-based treatment is best by far, but no matter how long you have lived with an eating disorder – if you are 20, 30, 40, 50 or 60 or more – you can regain quality of life. You can be free. Yes, you can. Reading *Anorexia Nervosa: A Recovery Guide for Sufferers, Families and Friends* and applying it to your life is a marvellous first step.

Pooky Hesmondhalgh

Years into recovery from anorexia, the bully still lurks. When I battled this illness I pushed everyone from me: family, friends, teachers. I didn't let anyone in; my only friend was the anorexia bully. People tried to help – especially at school. But there was no training in those days, no proven ideas on how best to help, so when I left the safety and support of school I was unprepared for the outside world. I lost a lot of weight during my first year at Oxford University.

With help from family and friends, I finally locked the anorexia bully out of my life. At the same time, I realised that school staff lacked eating disorder awareness and that I was the perfect person to provide this, so I embarked on a PhD. I hope that you'll find my contribution to *Anorexia Nervosa: A Recovery Guide for Sufferers, Families and Friends* (Chapter 17) useful.

Today I make positive decisions about my eating every day despite the bully's background presence. I have to – I've research to do, two beautiful daughters who need me, and a husband who loves me. No way will I let the anorexia bully waste more of my time.

About the illustrator

Elise Pacquette

Being an artist who understands the issues raised in this book (I know all about the bully inside the head), doing the illustrations has enabled me to utilise what was a 'potentially' negative experience and make it positive.

When I illustrated the first edition of this book in 1997, I was an in-patient under Professor Treasure. For years anorexia had been my identity, and this was one of the scariest things about recovery. Who would I be without it?

How did I let go of it? I found something I wanted more, a lot more. I found a career as a stage manager, which meant I had to start looking at my body as a 'tool' rather than 'my secret trophy of self-denial'. As a stage manager I had to be physically strong. Therefore, I had to make the painful choice to let go of my illness. And as I let go, I found that I could grasp hold of new things, new experiences; and I discovered life was more fun and a lot less lonely.

Fast forward to my identity today: a wife, a mum of two beautiful girls, a sign language interpreter, a cellist, a teacher, a painter, an illustrator, imperfect perhaps but good enough. Oh yes, recovery is worth the fight.

Acknowledgements

I am delighted that by joining with a team of highly creative and energetic people with lived experience of eating disorders it has been possible to update this book. We include some of the exciting new ideas that have been developed from research in eating disorders, particularly from our team at King's College, London, and the Maudsley Hospital. I hope that you find this new edition useful and inspiring.

Janet Treasure

One of the biggest delights of breaking free from an eating disorder and turning the tables on it, so to speak, by writing about it and raising awareness for others, has been the opportunity to meet and work with Professor Janet Treasure.

We co-edited *A Collaborative Approach to Eating Disorders* (2011) and then Janet suggested I help update her 1997 classic, *Anorexia Nervosa: A Survival Guide for Families, Friends and Sufferers*. This work has been very much the case of the researcher and survivor working together, combining and blending our experiences from each end of the eating disorder spectrum.

Writing *Anorexia Nervosa: A Recovery Guide for Sufferers, Families and Friends* has been a total pleasure, for along the way, in addition to working with Janet, I have met Pooky Hesmondhalgh and Elise Pacquette. Like me, Pooky and Elise have survived eating disorders. They are leading creative, talented and fulfilling lives, and each makes a valuable contribution to this update.

June Alexander

Introduction

You may be reading this book because you know or suspect you have anorexia nervosa and want to do something about it. Or you may be reading this because you suspect that someone you care about is suffering from anorexia nervosa. Even if the illness has been confirmed, you may be feeling confused and uncertain about how to respond. Perhaps you feel guilty and wonder if you somehow helped to cause the illness.

This book offers guidance for the way ahead. It has four sections. The first section gives a general outline of what anorexia is, what we believe causes it and a general historical perspective. The second section is for sufferers of anorexia nervosa and includes strategies to cope with and hopefully overcome the illness. The third section is for readers who want to help understand someone they care about (daughter, son, sister, brother, spouse, partner, friend) who has anorexia nervosa. Carers can be any of the above-mentioned important people in the sufferer's life but for convenience within this book, we usually refer to the carers as parents. The fourth section is for the professional person who wants to help or has been asked to help. This includes teachers, general doctors, counsellors, social workers, psychologists and psychiatrists. We encourage everyone to read each other's chapters. This is because the main focus of treatment is collaboration – that is, working together. There are no secrets here.

A major challenge in writing about anorexia nervosa is that the clinical picture is diverse. It can range from a mild transient episode, to a life-threatening illness or a chronic debilitating condition. It afflicts both males and females, in childhood, adolescence and adulthood.

You may find parts of this book of more interest than others. Select the topics that are relevant to your experience and situation. The section for sufferers comes first, before the section for carers, because we want to encourage you to reach out and grab the knowledge that this book provides, and be inspired and strengthened by it.

Carers, you can do a lot to help, especially by loving, and learning skills, and understanding what to say and what not to say, so that your actions and words are defusing rather than feeding the illness. But at the end of the day, the sufferers, encouraged by this care, have to be determined to dig deep, trust and find the will to fight for their life. Carers have an especially important role in helping child and adolescent sufferers reach the stage of recovery where they can regain independence, and even older sufferers usually require support before they are ready and able to fight off anorexia nervosa.

We suggest you approach this book by feeling free to skip passages and jump from section to section, to read what is most pertinent to your situation right now.

Anorexia nervosa is a terrifying illness, which can develop insidiously in children and adolescents, but also later in life. Relapse is common and constant vigilance is required to guard against this occurrence. Often, parents, friends, teachers and work colleagues know that something is wrong but don't know how to respond or what to do. This lack of information can be paralysing. As parents, you may be desperate to help but feel afraid of seeming interfering or intrusive. Accepting that your child has an illness with psychological connotations can be difficult. Many parents have problems deciding a joint plan of action because anorexia nervosa is out of the realms of their experience. Father may suggest one approach and mother another, and meanwhile the anorexia nervosa 'feeds' on this indecision and continues unabated.

Similarly, teachers may identify the symptoms of anorexia nervosa in a pupil but feel at a loss as to how to help. As a teacher, you may wonder how involved you should become. Is it appropriate for you to inform the parents and what should you say? How will you respond if the parents insist that nothing is wrong? How can you work with parents to arrange early intervention treatment, to do all you can to ensure that the anorexia nervosa doesn't take over their child? How can you help to integrate a pupil back into school after they have had time off with anorexia nervosa?

General practitioners may be confused over the best way forward for someone suffering from anorexia nervosa. As a GP, you may not always know if anorexia nervosa is the correct diagnosis. Even when the diagnosis is made, many health professionals may feel unsure how to help.

The aim of this book is to provide the necessary information about anorexia nervosa to enable you to recognise and address it. Importantly, although much hard work is usually required, everyone needs to remember that recovery is possible. Holding on to hope, and believing in recovery at all times, is essential.

The sooner the illness is recognised the easier it is to intervene to prevent it overcoming a life and becoming a way of life.

Section One

Anorexia nervosa:
an overview

1 What is anorexia nervosa?

A person with anorexia nervosa struggles to maintain a healthy weight. The illness occurs in both sexes but mainly in women. Mostly, it develops in childhood or adolescence and those affected feel terrified at the prospect of eating food and of gaining weight. Sufferers don't necessarily lose their appetite but become intensely anxious at the thought of consuming food. Their desire to lose weight differs to that of someone who goes on a hunger strike and stops starving if their goals are met. Sadly, for the person with anorexia nervosa, losing weight can become a way of life with no end point.

Understanding why eating or gaining weight can provoke such intense thoughts and feelings can be difficult. Most people cannot tolerate the physical pain, distress and misery associated with starvation and feeling hungry – especially when food is on hand.

The range of people who develop anorexia nervosa is diverse. Some sufferers have led tragic lives whereas, for others, anorexia nervosa appears to be the only blot on a happy life landscape. Here are some of their stories. Perhaps one or two will remind you of yourself or the person you know.

CASE EXAMPLES

Clare

I'm the middle child and have two brothers. My older brother was bright and intense, and I felt that my mother focused all her academic ambitions on him.

As for me, Mum seemed interested only in my appearance. When I was eight years old, she told me I was fat and seemed to be forever commenting on how much food I ate and on my shape. I never seemed to measure up to her expectations. I loved sport, but because the exercise made me hungry I gave it up and concentrated on dieting. I knew that, at some level, Mum loved me, but could not understand why she cared more about my size than my happiness. Eventually I decided that if I kept my weight down I would gain her acceptance and feel content, attractive and loved; instead I was always tired, irritable and hungry. Then I became too scared to eat even when I wanted to.

Stephen

I had been what you might call overweight since early childhood. At school, I coped with being laughed at and teased by becoming the class clown. I was an expert at being on the receiving end of 'fat' jokes. But that all changed at the age of 18 when, during a general consultation, my general practitioner asked if my family had a history of obesity. Suddenly, I stopped eating normally.

Jane

I was an only child and everything was fine until Mum died when I was 11. Dad relied on me quite a lot, and I looked after him and me for two years, when he remarried. Things changed then. Dad and my stepmother had a baby straightaway and, for the second time, I was left to fend for myself. I studied hard at school, but had few close friends. I moved out of the family home as soon as I could because the stress was awful. I did not feel wanted, and my stepmother encouraged me to find my own place to live. She seemed to want the house to herself with no memories of Mum and that, of course, included me. I became a nurse, married and gave birth to a beautiful daughter. I was feeling secure at last, but then I discovered my husband was having an affair. Yet again I felt dreadfully alone and bereft and this time became scared to trust anyone. At this point, I developed anorexia nervosa. The situation has worsened, with my parents-in-law having to look after my daughter because my illness has made me incapable of caring for her.

Beatrice

I enjoyed going to school and was the most popular girl among my class-mates. One girl became my best friend and someone started an online rumour that we were in love. This was hard to cope with, as I did not know who was behind the teasing. Then Dad was promoted in his job and our family moved cities. I was enrolled at a new school but felt lonely and unhappy. My younger brother seemed to have no problems settling into his new class – he played sport and soon had a fresh bunch of friends. I had always been a little overweight and sometimes overheard people in the street calling me 'Fatty' to my back. Mum had her own weight issues, and was enrolling at Weight Watchers. She could see I was not happy and invited me along to keep her company. I went with her and discovered that my weight fell off. I could not control what people said but now I was learning that weight was something I could control. Unfortunately, my diet led to anorexia nervosa and I became too afraid to eat even when I wanted to. When 17, I was referred by a general practitioner for extra help. I was extremely thin and unhappy during my first year at polytechnic but managed to complete the required credits.

Raj

I was an only child in an Indian family. Mum was a teacher and Dad was an engineer. I had been always been well liked at school and was academically successful, which pleased my parents. But I wished for a brother or sister with whom to play, talk and share experiences. I was one of the first boys in my class to go through puberty and became concerned when

I started having erections and sexual fantasies involving boys. Being shy, I did not feel confident enough to discuss these matters with Dad or my friends. I began to eat less and to work out for many hours on my rowing machine. This had the effect of making my sexual fantasies disappear so they were no longer an issue for me.

Jolene

My family was big, close and Catholic. For some reason, I felt smothered and wanted my independence. At age 16, I started dating an older man who made me feel special and kept me happy. Trouble was, within two years, I became pregnant by him. He insisted I have an abortion; otherwise he would end the relationship. His attitude shocked and horrified me, as an abortion was something I would never contemplate or do. The relationship ended and I went ahead with the pregnancy alone. My parents helped as much as they could but from early on in the pregnancy, I had difficulty eating due to nausea. This feeling of nausea has persisted, even though my son is now two years old. I am depressed, have no energy and feel embarrassed by my thin appearance.

Tom

I have had episodes of depression all my life. These dark moods usually responded to anti-depressants prescribed by my general practitioner. But one episode was different. Suddenly I found it very difficult to eat. Actually, I became afraid to eat. Food lay heavily on my stomach and it tended to repeat on me. I started vomiting to ease the horrid feeling that accompanied eating. Vomiting relieved the pressure and helped me feel more comfortable.

Samantha

I moved jobs and became anxious. Concerned that I would appear lazy, I increased my exercise routine and controlled my food intake. My weight fell rapidly as I developed anorexia nervosa.

A variety of different explanations are offered as reasons for not eating.

Kristine

I stopped eating at work in the belief that after lunch I was not as efficient.

Carol

> I developed rituals about food. I could not finish eating anything. I cut my food into tiny pieces and would leave half of it on the plate. Then I began to eat smaller and smaller amounts. Eventually, I ate nothing.

Trish

> All I could say was that eating gave me an uncomfortable feeling in my stomach and the only way to avoid that feeling and not feel anxious was to quit eating.

Kate

> I am definitely not suffering anorexia nervosa. I feel a fraud when people try to tell me that I have this illness. I mean, you have to be skinny if you have anorexia, and I'm not skinny. The doctors are trying to convince me otherwise, and my weight is dropping, but I know I'm still fat.

In most cases of anorexia nervosa, weight loss occurs as a result of exercise and a restriction of food intake. Other forms of weight control include vomiting and taking laxatives or diet pills.

The distinction between anorexia nervosa and bulimia nervosa (bingeing alternating with starving or vomiting) is often unclear. Some anorexia sufferers remain underweight and yet periodically gorge themselves. Mixed features of anorexia nervosa and bulimia nervosa multiply the medical problems associated with an eating disorder. Occasionally, very dangerous behaviours develop, such as those experienced by Paula.

Paula

> I developed anorexia nervosa when I was 12 after a change of school. My parents were keen for me to have a good education and sent me to an academically successful school in the next town. Most of my friends attended the more local school and I felt lonely. My parents became preoccupied at this time with my older sister's difficulties with a violent boyfriend. My weight fell rapidly. I was admitted to hospital but begged my parents to have me discharged early. At home I found eating difficult and started to binge. On one occasion I took an overdose of paracetamol which led to dramatic nausea and vomiting. After this episode, I regularly took six to eight paracetamol when feeling felt out of control. These pills produced

feelings of nausea, which enabled me to stop binge eating – for a short time, at least.

Anorexia can therefore include many different types of illness. The classic form of anorexia nervosa has been noted over several centuries, but in our current culture we are seeing a more diverse form of illness.

Understanding anorexia

As you can see from the case examples, anorexia nervosa is a complex illness. People with normal appetites may be unable to understand what is happening. One image that can be helpful is to imagine a 'bully' sitting inside the brain of the person with anorexia, manipulating their thoughts and taking over their willpower. This bully, which is very deceptive, is the anorexia nervosa.

Seeking help

Although the aim of this book is to provide information and ideas about ways that you can help, anorexia nervosa can be a severe illness with life-threatening complications, or may become very entrenched and last five years or more. Often, professional help is needed. Medical problems arise because of starvation and these need to be assessed by a doctor.

An important first step is to see your general practitioner, to discuss what additional help is required and how to access the necessary medical and psychological help. In some cases, intensive psychological help is required. Families are often seen together as they can play a major role in helping their loved one overcome the illness.

Anorexia nervosa is quite a rare illness. Many people misunderstand it and the sense of isolation and loneliness that occurs when facing the problem can make everything seem worse. Making contact with others who are experiencing the same illness, and also those who have recovered from it, can be a big help. An excellent way to do this is through support organisations (see page 161–163).

2 Avoid the blame game

Anorexia nervosa throws families into confusion. Living with someone who has anorexia nervosa can be difficult, as their behaviour may seem deliberately provocative and selfish. Remembering that the anorexia symptoms are an expression of unhappiness and distress can be difficult. Families may torment themselves wondering 'Where did we go wrong?' There are no simple explanations and asking this question will not help at all because parents do not cause eating disorders. A more helpful approach is to focus on how best to access and support treatment and to contribute to your loved one's recovery.

Remember, the person with the illness is also confused. On one level they can hear others begging them to 'snap out of it and just eat' but on another level the illness has convinced them that they cannot and must not eat, even if their life depends on it.

Anorexia nervosa often arises out of a complex mix of many factors. Rather than a simple 'A causes B', it is more like a pinball machine whereby a vulnerable person may bump into a variety of factors that change their life course and allow an eating disorder to start and *more* importantly take hold. The illness is definitely not:

- an indication that parents have gone badly wrong in raising their child
- a phase of silly, stubborn naughtiness
- something that sufferers can 'just snap out of'.

Having anorexia nervosa is a wretched, lonely experience. It is not a fad, a phase or a modern phenomenon. Historical medical records reveal that young women and men have had an illness remarkably like modern anorexia nervosa during the past four centuries (Chapter 3 deals with this in more detail). Although there is no overwhelming evidence that anorexia nervosa is increasing in frequency, evidence shows that it is becoming more difficult to overcome when it does arise. Our present culture, with an emphasis on thinness, tends to lock people into a career of anorexia nervosa.

We will outline some biological and environmental factors that appear to lead to anorexia nervosa. No one mechanism is responsible; instead, combinations of smaller factors, which in isolation are innocuous, appear to precipitate the problem.

The culture of thinness

Fashion

Some cultures predispose to anorexia nervosa. Western culture may increase the risk with its emphasis on thinness, skeletal super models and dieting behaviour as a norm for young women.

The number of young women presenting with eating disorders is increasing. The most marked increase is in people with binge eating (binge purge anorexia nervosa, bulimia nervosa and binge eating disorder).

Anorexia nervosa is less likely to be a 'slimming disease' than bulimia nervosa. Clearly, however, a slimming culture perpetuates the problem. Sometimes, a career choice exaggerates the need to be slim, as happened with Sarah:

Sarah

I was training at drama school to be an actress. My tutor drew me aside and said that I needed to control my weight as television work led to everybody looking bigger on the screen than in real life. So I immediately went on a diet and my weight fell. When I returned home to visit my parents they were shocked because I could hardly walk upstairs and had difficulty brushing my hair. They took me to the doctor and I was immediately admitted to hospital.

Self-control

Thinness is often regarded as a sign of mastery and self-control, regardless of how the control of body weight is achieved. This fashion for thinness is no different to any other cultural ideal of female beauty. For example, the bound 'lotus' feet of Chinese women were thought to be desirable. In fact they crippled women and led to chronic pain, and ill health. (Read further about this in the novel *Wild Swans* by Jung Chang). It is important to put this fashion for thinness into context.

Health

One message transmitted by the media is 'the lower the weight, the better the health'. This is not true. For mature women, the lowest levels of mortality are associated with a weight above that regarded as the 'normal' range. Also, the typical female pear-shaped distribution of fat, with a thin waist and rounded hips and thighs is not associated with any metabolic complications. Instead, the waist–hip ratio rather than weight is a better marker of risk, with the lower the ratio the better. A ratio of 0.75 is typical for women; a ratio of greater than 1 is associated with various health risks.

Treat messages about diet and health with caution. Extremely low fat diets may not be healthy, especially if used with other so-called healthy combinations, such as a no sugar or carbohydrate diet. Forget and ignore diet company advertisements that promise the world if only you will purchase their products. Instead, focus on eating three wholesome meals and three snacks every day to help keep eating disorders away.

Fear of food

Advice about healthy eating often becomes confused with the idea that certain foodstuffs such as sugars and fats are bad, but we need some of each to be healthy.

Scientific knowledge is incomplete and there are large swings in fashion. Twenty years ago carbohydrates were considered to be 'bad'. The pendulum has swung and carbohydrates are now 'good' whereas fats are 'bad'. The diet that is perceived to be 'good' may not have enough calories, leading to an intolerable hunger and overwhelming need to break the rules. To the best of our knowledge, it makes sense to aim to have a diet with less than 50 per cent fat. Generally speaking, there is no such thing as 'bad' or 'unhealthy' food although fresh home prepared foods are preferable to processed foods and drinks containing high levels of sugar, salt and fat; rather, it is best to eat a combination of foods, which together provide nutritional balance.

Food is now regarded with suspicion and fear. We are bombarded with warnings about eating too much of one food and not enough of another; advertisers encourage us to eat junk food and health authorities encourage us not to do so.

This constant bombardment in the media means that people who are vulnerable to compulsive worrying may become pre-occupied with the dangers that food contains and furthermore be at risk of developing an eating disorder. People who are more sensitive to threat and the opinions of others are more vulnerable to this influence. Also, people with a tendency to follow rules and structure with compulsive behaviours are at risk because they take warnings to heart and implement them.

A global backlash is developing against the culture of thinness and efforts are afoot to counteract the manipulative and exploitative forces of the giant diet food industries. The best we can do is to raise awareness about the risks and dangers of eating disorders, dispel the myths and educate others and ourselves with the facts.

It's all in the family, or is it?

Families, often without justification, blame themselves and feel guilty. Although you should tell your doctor or therapist about family or other difficulties that may be relevant, self or family blame is paralysing. Acknowledge and accept the past, whatever it has comprised, and focus your energy where it counts right now – on the present – and what you can do to aid recovery.

As parents, you may feel you are being pulled this way and that way. You see your child locked in behaviour patterns that are causing more and more problems. In Section Three we provide evidence-based tips on how you can help. Your support is needed and is critical for your child's health.

While searching for the causes within families is rarely productive, a focus on how family reactions and interactions can inadvertently keep the disorder going is of great value. We describe how to use the energy and love of families in a productive way in Section Three.

Genetic risk

There is a biological genetic risk to developing anorexia nervosa. It is not uncommon to have more than one affected member in the immediate family – a mother, grandmother or aunt may have had the illness. The vulnerability can come from either the maternal or paternal lines. Anorexia nervosa and obsessive compulsive disorder may share common genes.

Jenny

> I developed anorexia nervosa at the age of 17. My family recognised the symptoms, and realised that my behaviour resembled what had happened to my grandmother at the age of 15 in 1945. Grandma had lost weight when she was a schoolgirl. Her weight had fallen from 8 stone to 5 stone. The doctor had found nothing wrong with Grandma that could explain her weight loss. The doctor and the family became worried and admitted Grandma to a nursing home where she gradually gained weight after the nurses were able to persuade her to eat.

Research in the wider animal kingdom reveals not only instances where food preferences and body composition are under genetic control, but also conditions resembling anorexia nervosa. Young female pigs of certain stocks can suffer from a condition called 'thin sow syndrome'. Female pigs from these lines become locked into irretrievable emaciation. Their behaviour is similar to that seen in anorexia nervosa. They show a preference for low energy feed (straw) and become hyperactive and infertile. Lines of pigs that are bred for leanness are particularly at risk. Interestingly, stress triggers the problem.

We can conclude that some families have a genetic constitution that puts members at risk of developing anorexia nervosa. However, many other factors contribute to the onset and maintenance of the disorder.

The triggers

Stresses such as trauma, deaths or disappointments can trigger anorexia nervosa, particularly in the context of certain personality features. Being aware of these triggers is useful because anorexia nervosa may develop as a coping mechanism. However, this type of coping mechanism is dangerously deceptive. There is a sting in the tail of this form of coping – the sufferer may feel less anxious at first as the illness sets in, but anorexia nervosa thrives on being manipulative and sneaky. It leads to avoidance of the problem rather than finding an effective way of dealing with it. Therefore if we think of the big picture of life course, this form of coping is toxic. Importantly, early intervention may avoid much torment and pain – providing the right support and teaching coping skills may enable the child to process the event in a more adaptive and constructive way, and counteract self-defeating thoughts such as 'If I have a problem, I am bad/imperfect' or 'If I can't solve my problem straight away, then I must be inadequate'.

Stephen

As a teenager, I was enrolled at an all-boys boarding school. I had been slightly podgy before puberty but then I had a growth spurt and became tall and lean. I took up cross-country running, found I loved it and was winning some big races. However, a hip problem began to inflict severe pain and the doctor said I would have to give up running. I hoped the lay-off would not be for long but the pain continued and I had to have an operation. By this time I was very upset as running had been a major source of pleasure and provided a sense of accomplishment and connectedness among my friends who also enjoyed athletics. Things got worse instead of better. At about the same time I developed an ulcer on my penis. I was too embarrassed to discuss this problem with the matron at school and soldiered on for several days. Eventually the pain got so bad I called my mother who arranged an appointment with a general practitioner. Surgery was required. Afterwards I became withdrawn and unhappy. I was feeling depressed, out of things, no longer enjoying the company of the other boys and felt unable to take part in the usual fun and games. Instead I became obsessed with my weight and appearance. This seemed to help me cope. I started to avoid school meals and became preoccupied with fitness. I went on a variety of diets and bought books on slimming. My weight fell, though I did not think I was thin. But when my parents saw me, they were worried, and took me to the general practitioner who referred me to a psychiatrist.

Stephen's treatment included discussion on the loss of self-esteem caused by the inability to run and the painful embarrassment caused by the ulcer. He was able to explore these issues in therapy without worrying about appearing a wimp or needing to be macho. He was able to express his sadness and frustration that he would no longer be able to run. Problem-solving strategies enabled him to consider other activities which would provide pleasure and a sense of achievement without putting stress on his legs. He decided to take up rowing. During the revision time for his A-levels, he was able to stay at home where he was surrounded by support and love. Away from the teasing and competitiveness that flourished in the school environment, meals became much easier to eat. During the several months of therapy, Stephen grew 5cm and gained 20kg.

Susan

I developed anorexia nervosa after my grandfather died. I had been particularly close to him as we shared many interests. We loved the outdoors and he took me on fishing trips every weekend. I looked upon Grandpa almost as a father as Dad was frequently away from home on business trips or attending sport events with his mates. My parents had never got on well and I found it easier to talk to and confide in Grandpa – he always listened. When Grandpa died I was very sad but grieving for him was difficult as I felt that I had to be strong to look after Mum, who had more right to grieve and be upset than me.

Part of Susan's therapy was to grieve and come to terms with the loss of an important person in her life. This involved a long process of acknowledging the love and care that her grandfather had provided and, as a consequence, the loneliness and misery caused by his death.

Part of the normal grief response is to feel anger at the loved one for dying. People with anorexia nervosa often have difficulty accepting that they can be angry with people they love and so they block off or suppress this feeling. This prevents the normal emotional processing from taking place and the sufferer remains stuck as if the loss had just happened. Tears may spill out when talking about the event years later.

People who develop anorexia nervosa, on reflection, often can pinpoint an obvious trigger.

Margaret

I trained to be a nurse and had a good job in a London teaching hospital. Then my mother developed breast cancer and I was the obvious one in the family to be her prime carer. I had to fulfil this role in addition to my ordinary job and began to feel exhausted. Once or twice my professionalism slipped at work and I became irritated. To my horror, I also lost my cool at home and snapped at Mum. I was with her when she died and, although I knew it was hopeless, tried to resuscitate her. At the funeral I managed to appear calm and collected in looking after Dad and my sister. I didn't cry or break down, but carried on supporting my father during the next few months. At the same time my weight began to fall. When I began treatment, my mother's death and my difficulty in grieving for her were identified as important issues to work through.

Recovering from anorexia nervosa is hard work, with many fears to be overcome. When Margaret began to gain weight her anxiety increased. She became plagued by nightmares in which she relived the events surrounding her mother's death. At times she felt tempted to stop eating again as though this would make the torment go away.

Personal characteristics can be a risk

Perfectionism is a risk factor that appears in at least one part of the sufferer's life – such as tidiness, academic success or athletic prowess. The sufferer's drive for perfection may seem like an attempt to appease a self-critical part of themselves. A low opinion of the self is central and constant. The perfectionism therefore does not give pleasure but wards off pain.

This fragile sense of self is associated with a strong need to seek approval from others. Extreme external goals of success or achievement are set. For example, getting the top mark in the class, or exhibiting immense stamina in exercise training.

A tendency to value control over normal instincts and pleasures (head over heart) is another risk factor. This is the sort of personality that advocates the puritanical or selfless spirituality associated with asceticism in religion. The trait may come across in some people as stubbornness. It includes the beliefs that if you work hard you can overcome a problem, and that there is moral worth in trying to suppress or overcome your nature, including your need for food. Unfortunately, this characteristic, when combined with the 'Protestant work ethic' culture, can lead to setting unrealistic goals.

This wish for perfection and control and the belief that they are unobtainable or unworthy in some way, may also prevent people with anorexia nervosa from opening up to someone and talking about their difficulties. Also the ability to trust others is impaired. Our social brain is a high-maintenance tool and works inefficiently when not given fuel. This leads to problems decoding interactions and a bias to seeing others as a threat. Isolation and loneliness are a consequence and a barrier to obtaining the kind of emotional support known to be a factor in protecting people against developing psychological problems and, if such problems have evolved, in overcoming them.

3 Centuries of trying to understand food refusal

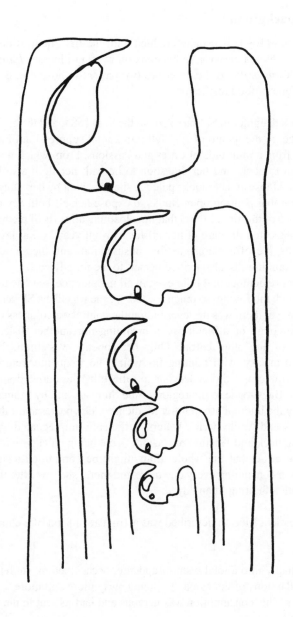

One of the most difficult things about coping with anorexia nervosa is the feeling of fear, anxiety, isolation and confusion. The problems associated with anorexia nervosa have been around for centuries. Early case examples help to illustrate the extent to which the difficulties you are experiencing, such as peculiar behaviours and unpredictable moods, are due to symptoms of anorexia nervosa, an illness. This chapter also reviews how the approach to treatment has evolved over time.

Historical background

Richard Morton (1694) is usually credited with the first medical description of patients with anorexia nervosa. In his book on wasting illnesses *Phthisiologia or a Treatise of Consumptions*, he describes two patients whose illness appeared to be due to voluntary food restriction:

> Mr Duke's daughter in St Mary Axe, in the year 1684, and the eighteenth year of her age, in the month of July fell into a total suppression of her Monthly Courses from a multitude of Cares and Passions. From which time her appetite began to abate and her digestion to be bad; her flesh also began to be flaccid and loose and her looks pale . . . she was wont by her studying at night and continuing pouring upon Books to expose herself both day and night to the injuries of the air . . . From that time loathing all sorts of medicaments she wholly neglected the care of herself for two full years, till at last brought to the last degree of a marasmus, or consumption, and thereupon subject to frequent fainting fits, she applied herself to me for advice.
>
> I do not remember that I did ever, in all my practice, see one that was conversant with the Living, so much wasted . . . she was like a Skeleton only clad with skin, yet there was no fever but on the contrary a coldness of the whole body; no cough or difficulty with breathing nor another distemper of the lungs or of any other entrail. Only her appetite was diminished and her Digestion uneasy, with fainting fits which did frequently return upon her. Which symptoms I did endeavour to relieve by the outward application of Aromatic Bags made to the region of the Stomack and by Stomack-Plaiters, as also by the internal use of bitter Medicine, Chalybeates and Juleps made of Cephalick and Antihysterick Waters, sufficiently impregnated with Spirit of salt Armoniack and Tincture of Castor . . . but being quickly tired with medicines she beg'd that the whole affair might be committed again to nature whereupon consuming every day more and more, she was after three months taken with a fainting fit and dyed.

The second patient Morton described was a 16-year-old son of a church minister who:

> fell gradually into a total want of appetite, occasioned by studying too hard and the Passions of the Mind . . . pining away more and more for a space of two years. This consumption was nervous and had its seat in the whole habit of the body.

This case was cured by advice which was to:

> abandon his studies, to go into the country air, and to use riding and a milk diet.

Another probable case of anorexia nervosa was Martha Taylor. She was a young girl from Derbyshire who ate no solid food for 12 to 13 months and lost so much weight that 'part of her belly touches her backbones'. She was visited by nobility and by several physicians. John Reynolds went to visit her on behalf of the Royal Society. He produced a report (1669) describing her case and others. He speculated on the cause of this phenomenon:

> Most of these Demoiselles fall to this abstinence between the age of fourteen and twenty years. Tis probably that the feminal humours in these virgins may be a long abode in their vessels grow acid. Her Age confirms the probability of a ferment in the feminals.

Unequivocal medical descriptions of anorexia nervosa appeared in the nineteenth century. Marce, a young French psychiatrist, wrote in 1860 of:

> young girls who at the period of puberty become subject to inappetancy car-ried to the utmost limited . . . these patients arrive at the delirious conviction that they cannot or ought not to eat. All attempts made to constrain them to adopt a sufficient regimen are opposed with infinite strategies and unconquer-able resistance. This behaviour persists until all traces of adipose tissue have disappeared and the patients are reduced to skeletons. They develop a weak-ness so great that they could scarcely walk a few steps. These unhappy patients only regain some amount of energy in order to resist attempts at ali-mentation . . . Some literally die of hunger but medical intervention can be most advantageous even when the patient seems devoted to incurability and death. I have seen three young girls thus cured who were reduced to a most alarming and almost desperate state. I would venture to say that the first phy-sicians who attended the patients misunderstood the true significance of this obstinate refusal of food: far from seeing in it a delirious idea of a hypochon-driacal nature, they occupied themselves solely with the state of the stomach.

Sir William Gull (a physician at Guy's Hospital) and Charles Lasegue (a French psychiatrist) between 1868 and 1888 brought the illness to the attention of the medical community with articles and case presentations. Lasegue's account is particularly vivid and well observed. He describes the lack of insight into the dangerousness of the weight loss and details all the excuses and reasons used to explain the refusal to eat:

> At first the patient feels uneasiness after meals, a vague sensation of fullness. The same sensations are repeated during the course of several days. They may be slight, but they are tenacious. She feels that the best remedy for this

indefinite discomfort will be to diminish her food intake. As yet there is nothing remarkable in her case. But gradually she reduces her food further and further and furnishes pretexts for so doing . . . By the end of a few weeks, there is no longer a temporary repugnance, but a refusal of food that may be indefinitely prolonged. The disease has declared itself . . . Meal after meal is discontinued and almost always some article of diet is successively suppressed.

Sometimes one food is replaced by another for which an exclusive predilection may be manifested. At first the general health does not appear to be aversely affected, and the constipation readily yields to mild laxatives. The abstinence tends to increase the aptitude for movement. The patient feels lighter and more active. She is able to pursue a tiring day without being aware of the lassitude of which she would at other times have complained. Both her family and her medical attendants become increasingly concerned, and the anorexia gradually becomes the sole preoccupation and topic of conversation. The patient no longer troubles herself to find an excuse for not eating. When told she cannot possibly live on the amount of food that would not suffice for an infant she replies that it furnishes sufficient nourishment for her adding that she had never refused to undertake any task or labour. She knows better than anyone what she requires, moreover it would be impossible for her to tolerate a more abundant diet . . . she says that she never was in better health and suffers in no way 'I do not suffer and therefore I must be well' is the monotonous formula which has replaced 'I cannot eat because I am unwell'. In fact the whole disease is summed up in this intellectual perversion.

Eventually, the tolerance of her economy, marvellous though it may be, is exhausted. The disease enters upon its third stage. Extreme emaciation occurs, general debility increases and exercise becomes laborious. The patient may now allow some re-feeding, but grudgingly with the evident hope that she will avert her peril without renouncing her ideas and perhaps the interest that her malady has inspired . . . I know patients who even ten years after the onset of their illness have not yet recovered the aptitude of eating like other people.

John Ryle a physician from Guy's Hospital, London, gave the Schorstein Lecture in 1936, which was later published in the *Lancet*. He presented his experience of 51 cases of anorexia nervosa seen over 16 years. He gave eight case histories to illustrate the various forms of the illness.

These descriptions are for the benefit of doctors and describe the physical symptoms. Below is the first case he describes.

Case 1
A girl aged 19 had been healthy and jolly in childhood, worked hard at school, matriculating at 16, and six months before went to France to learn the language. Just before she left home her periods previously regular stopped and she began to eat poorly. From that time she became steadily thinner. Except

for things containing vinegar and salads she had a dislike for all good food. Her mother was very worried and they clearly 'got on each other's nerves'. She was quiet and conscientious and liked her work in a bank. She complained of no symptoms. At home she was said to be happy as a rule, but sometimes nervy and irritable and apt to cry over the attempts to make her eat. Weight formerly 8st 10 lb now 6st 9 lb. Small undeveloped downy hair on face, arms and back, blotchy, red hands. Pulse 80, blood pressure 95/175. Treating at home in bed for a month her doctor secured a gain of 1.5 lb but the improvement was not sustained. In five months following the consultation again with home treatment after full explanation to the mother she gained 1st in weight. She then went back to her work and in the six subsequent years she never missed a day. Menstruation became normal within two months of the second course of treatment. She is now married and happy and has a healthy baby. Peripheral circulation remains poor.

These examples over three centuries apart have remarkable similarities to the way anorexia nervosa presents today. Not only is food refusal and extreme starvation a consistent feature but over-activity either physical or academic is an integral feature. A major difference from cases of today is that in none of these is fear of fatness or the pursuit of thinness given as a reason for not eating.

Time trends in treatment

One of the difficult aspects of anorexia nervosa is that there is no simple medical treatment such as a drug or an operation. Treatment has developed empirically based on clinical observation of what works. It is therefore of interest to note how treatment has developed over time and what the outcome and prognosis was and to compare it with current treatment and outcomes.

Most of the authors who describe cases also discuss their treatment. Richard Morton (1694) gave this advice:

> Let the patient endeavour to divert and make his mind cheerful by exercise, and the conversation of his friends. For this disease does almost always proceed from Sadness and Anxious Cares. Let him also enjoy the benefit of an open, clear and very good Air, which does very much relieve the nerves and spirits. And because the Stomach in this Distemper is principally affected a delicious diet will be convenient, and the Stomach ought not to be long accustomed to one sort of food.

Marce (1860) was struck by how difficult it was to implement treatment at home, and he therefore advised:

> The hypochondriacal delirium, then, cannot be advantageously encountered so long as the subjects remain in the midst of their own family and their

habitual circle: the obstinate resistance that they offer, the sufferings of the stomach, which they enumerate with incessant lamentation, produce too vivid an emotion to admit of the physician acting with full liberty and obtaining the necessary moral ascendancy. It is therefore indispensable to change the habitation and the surrounding circumstances and to entrust the patients to the care of strangers.

It is necessary to proceed progressively and by degrees. Each day at each repast the nourishment be it liquid or solid, should be gradually increased. As to exercise and gymnastics, which are commonly recommended, they have the inconvenience of a great expenditure of energy, which the daily alimentation is unable to withstand. These patients will be seen to undergo a great change and their strength and condition to return and their intellectual state to be modified in a most striking manner . . . but relapses are in these cases easy.

Gull's (1874) advice was similar. He also acknowledged the importance of focusing on the primary goal of treatment, which was to restore adequate nutrition by not succumbing to the sufferer's explanations and protestations. He was confident that the problem lay in the mind and that the patient's reasoning and logic was at fault:

In reference to treatment the patients require moral control: and that, if possible a change in domestic relations should be made. From the beginning food should be given at short intervals and that patients should not be left to their own inclination in the matter. The inclination of the patients must in no way be consulted. In earlier and less severe cases it is not unusual for the medical attendant to say in reply to the anxious solicitude of the parents, *'Let her do as she like. Don't force food'*. Formerly I thought such advice admissible and proper but larger experience has shown plainly the danger of allowing the starvation process to go on . . . patients should be fed at regular intervals and surrounded by persons who would have moral control over them: relatives and friends being generally the worst attendants.

As regards prognosis, none of these cases, however exhausted are really hopeless whilst life exists, and for the most part the prognosis may be considered favourable. The restless activity referred to is also to be controlled but this is often difficult.

Gull illustrated his paper with a case example of a girl, Miss C, 15 years 8 months whom he had been asked to see. His notes state:

C ailing for a year and become extremely emaciated. Very sleepless for six months hence. Lower extremities oedematous. Mind weakened. Temper obstinate. Great restlessness.

Gull wrote to her doctor advising him on her management:

> Dear Dr Andersen,
> I saw Miss C today. The case appears to be an extreme instance of what I have
> proposed to call Apepsia hysterican or Anorexia Nervosa. I would advise warm
> clothing, and some form of nourishing food every two hours as milk, cream,
> soup, eggs, fish or chicken. I must only urge the necessity of nourishment in
> some form otherwise the venous obstruction which had already begun to show
> itself by oedema of the legs will go on plugging off the vessels. With the nour-
> ishment I would conjoin a dessertspoonful of brandy every two or three hours.
> Whilst the present state of weakness continues, fatigue must be limited and if
> the exhaustion continues the patient should be kept in a warm bed. . .
> Yours truly,

Gull obtained a letter from her doctor six months later reporting on progress:

> Dear Sir William,
> Miss C is at Shanklin but returns soon.
> The great difficulty was to keep her quiet, and to make her eat and drink.
> Every step had to be fought. She was most loquacious and obstinate, anxious
> to exert herself bodily and mentally.

The last report was one year later:

> Dear Sir William,
> I am sure you will be delighted to hear that Miss C in whose case you were so
> kindly interested has now made a complete recovery and is getting plump and
> rosy as of yore.

In the 1890s, Pierre Janet, an eminent French psychiatrist, wrote of the difficulties
in managing these cases. He followed Lasegue and conceptualised the illness in
three phases. He called the first a gastric phase in which everyone assumed that
there was an affliction of the stomach. He, however, noted that this first phase was
more often the consequence of an emotion. The second phase was when the family
become alarmed:

> Now they try to allure the patient by all possible delicacies of the table, they
> scold her severely, they alternately spoil, beseech, threaten her. The excess of
> the insistence causes an exaggeration of the resistance; the girl seems to
> understand that the least concession on her part would cause her to pass from
> the condition of a patient to that of a capricious child, and to this she will
> never consent.
> All the relatives and friends interfere by turns to try what their authority
> and influence may do. The girl repeats that she is never hungry, that she does
> not need more food, that she can live indefinitely in that way, that, moreover

> she has never felt better . . . our strange patient struggles with all those around her by every possible means. She seeks a support in one of her parents against the other, she promises to do wonders if her family are not too exacting, she has recourse to every artifice and every untruth.

The third phase was when physical problems developed. Janet suggested that a proportion became frightened at this and would begin to eat but he noted that a subgroup continued to refuse to eat even at this terminal phase.

Janet was fascinated by the refusal to eat and by the over-activity that he recognised as part of the condition. He did not think that the over-activity was a secondary feature; rather, he thought a core feature of anorexia nervosa was a strange feeling of happiness, a euphoria in which state the need for food, feelings of weakness and depression disappeared.

John Ryle (1936) did not insist that the sufferer from anorexia nervosa had to be separated from her home surroundings. Rather, he suggested that good results could be obtained at home:

> if the situation is clearly and fairly explained to the patients and (especially in the case of the younger subjects) to the parents also, and if co-operation with the family doctor is maintained by them.

He went on to state that it was useful to explain to the patients and parents separately the nature of the disease in the simplest and most direct terms. He recommended a strong assurance be given that recovery would take place once the starvation habit was corrected and the appetite restored by giving the stomach a sufficient intake of nourishing food to maintain not only the bodily requirements but also its own efficiency, of which appetite was a normal expression. The absence of organic disease had to be confidently expressed. Parent and child needed to see that the physician had a complete grasp of the situation.

If the programme initiated at home was not proceeding satisfactorily, treatment was better carried out in a nursing home. Doctor and nurse needed to obtain early and full control over the patient and from the beginning ensure that the food provided was eaten. In some cases it would be necessary to sit with the patients until each meal is finished. Firmness, kindness and tact were to be used in just proportions and the nurse could not let herself be wheedled into concessions. A mixed diet from the beginning was preferable. It had to be remembered that some patients were capable not only of declining food but also of hiding and disposing of it and even of inducing vomiting when the nurse's back was turned. Direct inquiries into motive and difficulties were better avoided, at any rate in the earlier stages and in the youthful cases. Explanation, reassurance, distraction and firm treatment of the starvation were usually adequate and would ensure a steady and parallel improvement in the mental and physical states. Not uncommonly, waywardness or periodic emotionalism or a subdued or alternatively a bossy attitude of mind would persist after physical recovery but this was hardly to be regarded as a continuation of the disease.

Hilda Bruch was a psychoanalyst in America who developed a special interest in anorexia nervosa. She also emphasised the need to address the starvation as a priority. In the Founders Award Lecture for the American Psychiatric Association Meeting in 1981 (Bruch, 1982), she charted the development of her ideas. She had been struck by the fact that traditional psychoanalysis was rather ineffective. She ascribed part of the treatment difficulties to polarised models of treatment. She contrasted those that concentrated on weight gain only with complete disregard of the psychological problems with psychoanalysis extending over several years with disregard for the low weight.

For effective treatment, changes and corrections must be accomplished in several areas. The patient's nutrition must be improved, the tight involvement with the family needs to be resolved and the inner confusion and misconceptions require clarification. The patient's persistent malnutrition creates psychological problems that are biologically not psychodynamically determined. The fact is that no true picture of the psychological problems can be formulated, nor can psychotherapy be effective, until the worst malnutrition is corrected and the patient becomes capable of assimilating and processing new information.

Bruch developed a method of treatment that involved active collaboration between patient and therapist. She first explained her conceptualisation of the illness:

> The preoccupation with eating and weight is a cover up for underlying problems and patients' doubt about their self worth and value, that they need help to discover their good qualities and assets and that at this stage the severe starvation interferes with their psychological processes. It is important to clarify from the outset that the goal of psychotherapy is to accomplish something for the patient's benefit and not to appease the parents.
>
> In a way, all anorectic patients have to build up a new personality after all the years of fake existence. They are eternally preoccupied with the image they create in the eyes of others, always questioning whether they are worthy of respect. There is a basic mistrust which permeates all relationships – the conviction that all people look down on them with scorn and criticism and that they have to protect themselves against this. This mistrust is usually hidden from the therapist under the facade of pleasing co-operation, at least initially. Sooner or later this will be succeeded by criticism and negativism and then by open hostility.

You can see from this brief history of treatment that the approach we outline in this book follows from that advocated by these luminaries in the field. A main tenet of treatment was for the doctor to share their understanding of the illness with the patient and the family and then to help them withstand the difficulties they would encounter correcting the malnutrition. Although they all understood the psychological underpinnings of the condition, the doctors also realised that they had to attend to the physical aspects of the illness as a priority. We hope that the information and suggestions that we provide will build on Hilda Bruch's concept of active collaboration. For active collaboration, people with anorexia nervosa need information and help. It is difficult in a book, however, to tailor the information to suit each person. Therefore, some parts of the book may seem too technical, some parts may seem obvious and yet others may seem irrelevant. We suggest that you look through the whole text and focus on areas that are most helpful for you.

Section Two

For sufferers

4   Starting the recovery journey

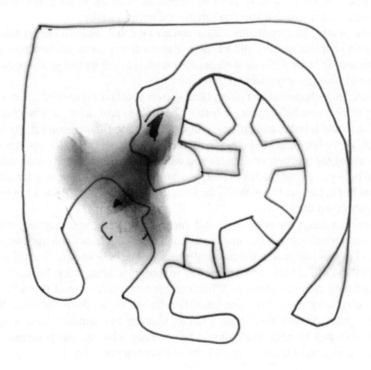

Recruiting help

Section Two is primarily for the sufferer – especially for people who feel ready to regain their true self and be free of their anorexia nervosa bully. You may be fortunate to be able to work through this section with professional help. Some chapters in Sections One and Three also will be relevant to you. For example, you may be interested to understand the causes of the illness outlined in Section One.

Section Three describes the stages you need to go through when trying to come to grips with and understand your anorexia nervosa. Perhaps you are reading this book because you are in the contemplation stage; that is, you think you might have a problem but are undecided. Alternatively, you may have reached the action stage where you need as much help as you can get, as you are fighting on all fronts. There again, you may be in the pre-contemplation stage and reading this because someone asked you to, but you don't think you have a problem.

Whatever stage you are at, this section contains the tools you need to get moving and regain your true identity and freedom. Parents and concerned others may also find this section helpful. The first stage of the work is to ensure that you understand as much as possible about what is going on.

We need to be honest at this point. Getting over anorexia nervosa often involves getting much worse before you get better. The illness seems to sense when people are on to it, and it bucks and creates a ruckus, hoping to frighten you off. So hang in there, be vigilant and hold steadfastly on to hope at all times. Remember that this is one of the toughest challenges you will ever face. People may have said to you, 'If only you would eat this or that, you would be better'. In the long term they are right but in the short term this is far from the truth. An eating disorder is about much more than food.

Recovery takes a lot of courage and energy. Physically, you may feel awful, your stomach and gut may become bloated and sore, your bones and muscles may ache and psychologically and emotionally you will be on a seesaw. We will work through these difficulties in more detail as we progress through this book.

Negotiating recovery alone is difficult and we therefore suggest that you find someone (ideally more than one person) with whom to share the task. Your recovery guide doesn't have to be a family member but someone who is often highly motivated to help. They should be someone who can see you regularly. Here is a checklist of qualities to look for in choosing your helper.

Support questionnaire

Could 'X' be your support? Answer the following questions.

1.   How easy is it to talk to X about your problem?

Very easy (5 points)
Quite easy (4 points)
Not sure (3 points)
Quite difficult (2 points)
Very difficult (1 point)

2. Is X critical or easily upset about your eating? Does X take your eating behaviour personally?

   Always (1 point)
   Often (2 points)
   Sometimes (3 points)
   Rarely (4 points)
   Never (5 points)

3. Could you talk to X even if you weren't making progress?

   Definitely (3 points)
   Not sure (2 points)
   Definitely not (1point)

4. Can you trust X to be always there when you need someone – with no strings attached? No moral blackmail?

   Definitely (5 points)
   Probably (4 points)
   Maybe (3 points)
   Probably not (2 points)
   Definitely not (1 point)

5. When you overcome your anorexia, what will X's likely response be?

   X may feel threatened by this. They will have to find a new role and way of living (0 points)
   X may feel lost and slightly jealous that I can become more independent and successful with my life (0 points)
   I haven't a clue (1 point)
   X will be very pleased for me (2 points)

6. How often are you in contact with X?

   At least once a week (3 points)
   At least once a fortnight (2 points)
   At least once a month (1 point)
   Less than once a month (0 points)

Total points 19–23: You are in the lucky position of having a near perfect supporter nearby. Definitely invite person X to help you in your efforts to overcome your eating disorder.

Total points 12–18: It is uncertain whether X should be your supporter. Possibly, this person is too emotionally involved to be helpful. They may not be able to cope with the ramifications.

Total points 4–11: Look for someone else or go it alone.

> *We suggest that you ask your chosen helper to read Section Four. It is easy for helpers with the best will in the world to fall into a trap set up by the anorexic bully and hinder rather than help change.*

Phase one: first steps

The most difficult step is to let yourself realise, acknowledge and accept that you have an illness. If you have not done so already, we suggest you read some of the chapters in Section One, especially the historical one (Chapter 3). You will note an integral feature of anorexia nervosa is that sufferers often think they don't have a problem. That is, you probably do have anorexia nervosa if others are worried about you but you are not worried about yourself! Eventually, most sufferers reach the stage when they recognise that the anorexia bully has strangled their life and they long to be free. At first this idea comes and goes.

Doing anything about overcoming your anorexia is difficult until you fully accept that your anorexia is a concern for you. This chapter will help you reach this stage.

One concept that we have found useful is to conceptualise anorexia nervosa as a 'bully' that sits in your brain and whispers instructions and orders to you about how to behave and cope with a situation. Hold this thought and think about your illness as something that does not have your best interests at heart and is separate from your true self.

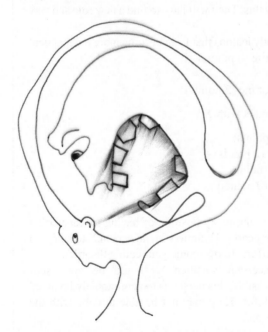

The anorexia bully

You will find it helpful to start working out which thoughts and behaviours belong to the bully, and which belong to the real you. This helps you to start seeing the illness for what it is – and to start working on dismantling it. Picture this manipulative bully in the 'schoolyard' of your mind. How does it make you think? How does it make you feel? How does it make you behave? Write down your thoughts. Do you have an image, other than a bully, that makes more sense to you? Focus on this for a while. Write about or draw it.

Seeing how other people set about this task may help you get started. For example:

Julie

I was aged 28 when I decided enough was enough. I had developed anorexia nervosa four years earlier. I decided to seek treatment because my boyfriend and I had become more committed to each other. I wanted treatment for my anorexia nervosa before our relationship went further. After my first session with the therapist I took the image of the anorexia bully home with me and started to work on it. I structured the way the anorexia bully was affecting my health (physical and psychological) and the way it was affecting my social life (career and family).

How the anorexia bully affects my physical health

1. I'm exhausted all the time and end up falling asleep during the day for a few hours.
2. When I'm working out, my body and muscles are telling me to stop, but I won't. My eating disorder thoughts drive me on.
3. I have headaches all the time. This may be because of dehydration.
4. I feel light-headed all the time. I feel faint if I get up too quickly.
5. I don't sleep well at nights. I keep waking up every hour.
6. I look pale most of the time.
7. When I've eaten I feel so full that my stomach is distended. I'm afraid to look at it.
8. I get constipated sometimes.
9. Having a dry mouth all the time makes me feel weak and dirty. I'm always cleaning my teeth.
10. I feel weak and listless all the time and seem to have no energy – even though I drive myself to do the physical workouts.
11. Sometimes I feel my arms and legs are just too heavy to lift.
12. I get aches in my joints all the time.

How the anorexia bully is affecting my psychological health

1. I feel I'm too fat even though people tell me that I am thin. But I can't see it. I know they are lying and saying I look thin to make me feel better. Well, I don't feel better. I am fat, fat, fat.

2. I have to exercise constantly otherwise I'll have extra blobs of fat where I don't want them. I feel very guilty and annoyed with myself if I don't exercise a certain number of times each week. Each day, actually.
3. I am very controlled about my diet. I feel guilty just for eating. I get panicky about it.
4. I feel the need to be very strict with myself – I have rules and I have to live by them to feel I can cope and get through each day.
5. I feel tearful most of the time. I feel I am putting on a front to show people I am fine. I am ashamed of how I feel inside. I'm so weak, always letting myself down.
6. I'm very unhappy about myself. I hate myself and get depressed, wondering how much longer I can go on.
7. I don't have enough enthusiasm for things anymore. I used to be enthusiastic about everything. My day is consumed with the number of calories I can eat for the day and the amount of exercise I must do to alleviate my anxiety.
8. I don't have the get up and go I once had. Everything is such an effort now.
9. I have to write everything down as I have trouble remembering things.

How the anorexia bully has affected my career

1. I work part time at the moment because I'm not fit or strong enough to work full time. I work in the morning when I'm at my best. In the evenings I'm exhausted from trying to meet the demands of my illness.
2. My career development has been put on hold.

How the anorexia bully affects relationships

1. Mother constantly tells me I need food, but I ignore her and eat nothing. She gets angry but I'm afraid to eat and feel better if I don't eat. If I do eat, I feel guilty and have to do more exercise to compensate. I try to keep busy and shut out the food thoughts but they keep bothering me.
2. I have lost interest in sex with my boyfriend, although I think about it quite often. I don't want him to see my body and see how big I am. Also I dread him hugging or touching me in case he feels some fat. I don't want him put off for life.

How the anorexia bully has affected friendships

1. Before this illness I had a lot of friends but now I hardly see them because I'm too exhausted to go out at night. Sometimes they come round to visit me.
2. If I've agreed to see them, I start to worry and want to cancel, thinking I won't enjoy it. Once they arrive, I do enjoy myself but being in the moment, focusing on conversations taking place around me, takes so much effort. Yet my friends are very important to me.

3. I have to psyche myself up to see them. I have to get into the mood/right frame of mind. It is so easy to listen to the eating disorder 'voice' in my head, which wants me to be alone and go nowhere.
4. I miss out on a lot of fun and many social occasions because I avoid eating out with my friends. Eating in front of others makes me very anxious so I pretend I have something else on, and stay home, alone with my bossy eating disorder thoughts. I worry that my friends will not understand that my behaviour is due to fear and will give up on me.

Do you recognise and identify with any of these thoughts? Can you add to these lists?

While you are at this stage, another useful exercise is to write several letters. First, write a letter to your anorexia nervosa bully as if it were your enemy. Tell it exactly what you think of it. Accuse it of causing you problems, which it most certainly has done, and be explicit. What troubles has it pulled you into? Jackie wrote the following letter.

Jackie's letter

Dear Anorexia (my enemy),
You have been dogging every hour of my life for more than 10 years. You were with me during all my student days. You made it difficult for me to join in with everyone else. You wanted me all to yourself. I tended to withdraw from opportunities to have fun with friends, especially if they were going out for a meal, saying that I needed to study. I passed my exams with distinction but, due to your domination, I didn't make any friendships that are still with me. Also I don't seem to be getting on at work now I've qualified. I feel like I am on the periphery of what is happening rather than really part of things. I find it difficult to concentrate and I sometimes miss the point.

All of my peers at college are now marrying and having babies. I have never had a relationship, however fleeting. I guess I have spent all my time thinking inwards, listening to you, instead of engaging with the outside world. I can see now that I have isolated myself under your influence. No wonder men don't seem interested in me. Anyway, I'm frightened to get too close to the opposite sex in case they suspect my secret – I mean, I would not want to tell them about us; I'm pretty sure they would up and run; perhaps they can sense there's something not right, anyway.

Everything is a struggle. I'm exhausted all the time. And cold. I need layers of clothes on, trying to keep warm, especially in the winter. I feel hopeless when I think about the future – isolated, lonely, irritable and unwell. It's not as if I expect too much out of life – a companion, a home and a job, that's all. I see it all so clearly now. You have sabotaged the lot.
Yours with regret and anger, Jackie

How do you feel reading Jackie's letter? What feelings do you think she experienced when she wrote it? You will find it helpful to write your own letter – it will help you see your anorexia for what it is – an illness that you developed and has overtaken most if not all areas of your life. If you haven't written your letter yet, go and do it now.

How did you feel writing a letter to your anorexia bully enemy? Can you show your letter to someone you trust and seek their comments? Would they want to add any more ways that the illness has impacted on your life?

Another way to focus on the current situation is to take yourself to the future, say five years on, when you are still struggling to live each day with anorexia nervosa. Write a letter to a friend describing what your life is like then. How does it make you feel? Show it to a friend. Is this what you really want?

Of course not! The good news is that you can regain your own true self, and live a full and rewarding life, free of your eating disorder.

Giving up anorexia will not be easy. Once you have made the decision to struggle with your anorexia bully it will kick up a fuss and try to convince you that it knows best. You will have numerous questions, anxieties and fears. You may think you should suppress some because they sound silly or unimportant, but however silly or trivial they may seem, share them with your recovery guide and deal with them straightaway – otherwise they may expand and bowl you over later. Recovering from anorexia nervosa is difficult. Quite possibly this will be the most difficult challenge you will ever face. Maybe, like many others, you have tried before, and failed. Importantly, keep trying. Never give up! Perhaps previous recovery attempts were based on misconceptions. Things may be different now. Reading this book is a good start. You may have other helpful resources too. Try to focus on eliminating possible obstacles to your recovery.

Phase two: struggling with recovery

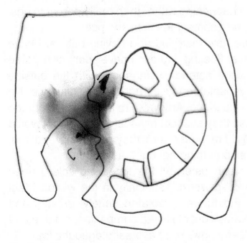

Confronting the anorexia bully

Annabel describes the work that she undertook when preparing to tackle the struggles involved in recovery.

Annabel

Annabel was 17. She had developed anorexia nervosa at the age of 13. She had missed two years' school. Her younger sister was very fed up with the attention and disruption that the anorexia had caused the family. Annabel wrote down her thoughts on contemplating the drawing that shows her bossy illness is part of her but not her true self.

How shaking off the anorexia bully will affect my psychological health

1. I will be scared that if I start eating that I won't be able to stop.
2. I will get out of control.
3. How will I cope with gaining weight and not exercising? Will the weight go on mainly as fat and not as muscle?
4. I will be frustrated that I am not completely better. I *should* be better.
5. I may become more distressed. I often deal with stressful situations by increasing my rituals and compulsive actions.

How shaking off the anorexia bully will affect my physical health

1. I might feel very bloated.
2. Gaining weight, I will worry about my body shape.

How shaking off the anorexia bully will affect my social life

1. Remarks, based on ignorance, may be made about fattening-up nicely – *'Annabel, you are looking well!'*
2. I may need support from people who can help me strengthen my true sense of self, and at the same time avoid those people who trigger anorexia thoughts.
3. I may start re-connecting with lots of feelings that have been suppressed by my illness, and this may take a lot of adjusting to do.
4. I may feel embarrassed and not want to see friends when I am in this in-between stage.
5. This illness is in my brain – I know this, but if I am no longer really thin, I'm afraid people will consider me recovered and expect me to behave normally, like eating with others and dining out, when I am not ready to do so.

How will shaking off the anorexia affect my career?

1. I may have some self-doubt and wonder if I am clever enough.
2. Even though I know it is dreadfully false, I will have to work on building up my confidence to avoid wanting to use the anorexia as a prop.

How will shaking off the anorexia bully affect relationships with my family?

1. A tiny part of me – the illness part, no doubt – thinks I am being weak by letting go of my anorexia, and that I am giving in to my parents. However, as my true self, I know I am strong rather than weak to confront my fear of eating, and my parents will be pleased to know I want to put on weight too.
2. My parents get impatient and think I'm not gaining weight fast enough and it's worse when they don't acknowledge this verbally – they simply go all silent. My mum, especially, rejects passively. She can make me feel guilty without saying anything. I need encouragement rather than silent criticism to help me beat this thing.
3. My emotions – with which I am totally out of touch – may well up and explode like a volcano. For instance, if I feel misunderstood by something I say, or if I am accused of being uncommunicative when inwardly I am trying my hardest to defuse anorexia thoughts, I may explode and take it out on my family and become very angry. I am going to need lots of patience and understanding while I learn to get in touch with my feelings and express them in a healthy way.

Do items on this list ring true for you? What others can you add? How do you feel, thinking about all the things that will be difficult if you go for recovery?

Another way to concentrate your mind on the issues that you will miss when you give up anorexia nervosa is to write a letter to the anorexia bully, your friend. Anne wrote the following letter.

Anne's letter

> Dear Anorexia (my friend),
> With you I know where I am. You are with me 24/7 and you never let me down. With you in my life, I know what to think and say. I get a high from remaining in control. It's good to feel special and different and not bothered by things that seem to distract so many others. With you I don't feel lonely, I know how to cope with stressful situations at home, with my studies and at work. You are even with me in the evenings. Whenever I want you, you are here – for me and only me. You convince me that I am safe with you. Your way of life is so familiar and you are so much part of me, how can I ever lose you?
> With love, Anne

How does this letter make you feel? What would you say to Anne to comfort her about the loss of her anorexic 'bully friend'?

You may find it helpful to write a letter to your anorexia 'bully friend', too. We suggest you take time out to write the letter now. Don't hold back!

OK, assuming you have written your letter to your anorexic 'friend', how did you feel when you wrote this letter? Can you show it to your recovery guide? Be brave, go ahead and do so. What do they say about it?

Finally, you need to consider what your life will be like when you leave your anorexia behind. Quite likely, you stepped straight from childhood and into anorexia nervosa. You therefore have missed out on a most valuable stage of development – your teenage years. Teenage years are useful for exploring different attitudes and behaviours before settling down to your adult self. It can be very frightening to have missed out on this transition stage and to have to pick up an adult persona without preparation. The good news is that with your recovery guide by your side, you can learn skills to help you adapt and enjoy catching up on the life you have missed out on. Look forward to fun and adventure.

Phase 3: what to expect with recovery

What do you imagine life will be like when you are free of the anorexia bully? Allow yourself to dream. What images come to your mind? Write them down and draw them.

Helen

Helen developed anorexia nervosa at 19 when she left home to train as a radiographer. She became so weak, she was forced to leave her course and returned to live at her parents' home. Here are some of the things that Helen began to think about when contemplating recovery.

What will happen to my social life when I leave my anorexia bully behind?

1. People will no longer worry about me.
2. I will be able to complete my studies, find employment and be more independent.
3. I might feel left out and forgotten about again.

What will happen to my psychological health when I leave the anorexia bully behind?

1. I accept that I will not feel good about myself. I have no idea what thoughts will replace those of the bully which has dominated my mind for so long. I will have to cultivate new interests and pastimes to fill the gap.
2. I will feel very concerned about my body shape, especially when watching TV, or looking at images in magazines or online. It will be tempting to make comparisons and I fear I will feel fat and horrible. That said, I know that body image is not what really matters, and will practise deleting the bully's triggers with strong self-talk. Freedom to be me, without the bully's torment, is what really matters.

What will happen to my physical health when I leave my anorexia bully behind?

1. I won't be cold and tired any more.
2. I'll get my periods back and start to look and feel like a normal woman for the first time.
3. My hair and skin will start to look healthy.
4. My teeth will be in better shape.

Preparing for the rest of your life

Knowing what you want, when you have had to carry the burden of anorexia for a long time, can be difficult. Can you imagine what life can be like without anorexia nervosa? It's difficult to step outside the small world, that is the anorexia prison, to see what will be there. One way to focus your mind is to write a letter to a friend describing the future in five years, imagining all is well and you have got rid of your anorexia nervosa. If you are having difficulty thinking about five years, shorten the interval to two years, one year or this afternoon! Start now!

Helen wrote the following letter to her friend Susan.

Helen's letter

Dear Susan,
It's difficult to look back and contemplate all the changes that have taken place in my life during the past few years. You will remember that I was deeply morose and desperate when a prisoner of my anorexia nervosa.

Rather than mourn the loss of those years, I focus on knowing that I have learnt a lot from my illness. In a liberating sort of way, the recovery process has helped me to deeply value life and all it offers. The work I have done in regaining my true self has given me a chance to make a fresh start and to do what feels right for me – in the past I tended to do what I thought was expected of me. For instance, I had decided to study radiography because I thought this would please my mother who had trained as a nurse. However, I had never been very good at science and found the rote learning of anatomy dreadfully difficult and uninteresting.

I have learnt that I need to do things to please me rather than try to get other people's approval which I never seemed to achieve no matter how hard I tried. I therefore enrolled in a graphic design course and then I started to live. I still probably work too hard but I always feel purposeful and fulfilled. I get a big thrill to see my designs promoting products, and am forever trying new and exciting techniques. Working in an environment with like-minded people is uplifting.

Another major lesson I have learnt from my illness is the need to trust others and give them the space and opportunity to show their friendship.

I am able to open up a little and share my bad times as well as my good. It's great to realise that people don't think I am selfish or boring if I tell them how I really feel. I have found that any dark moments vanish after a little sympathy and humour. Laughter, I have discovered, is one of life's best feel-good tonics. Sharing time with friends and family is as precious and important to me as time in my graphic art studio.

I guess many people will think that my eating habits remain a little on the weird side but I ensure that my size 12 clothes never get too loose on me. I've abandoned scales, diets and cults of thinness. I have no diet foods in my refrigerator and feel healthier for it.

My relationship with my parents has improved. I know that they don't approve totally of my lifestyle but we have tacitly agreed to disagree. I am not the person they dreamed their child would be and, importantly, I no longer care. What really matters is that I am true to me. Not true to my eating disorder, or my parents, but me! This attitude makes all the difference between coping and not coping. I recognise and respect that my parents have a right to choose how they live their life and equally I have a right to choose how to live mine. As for my eating disorder, any traces are relegated to the furthest recesses of my mind, where they are totally negated.

Let's catch up for lunch soon!

Hugs,

Helen

Let yourself daydream. Imagine you have three wishes. What would you like to happen if you didn't have anorexia nervosa? Once you can imagine your life without anorexia nervosa, practise getting into this fantasy each day. At first, just practise doing it while you are lying in bed. Go back to the same scene each night and add to your image. Make it exactly how you want it. How does the image make you feel? If you feel slightly frightened or distressed bring a friend into your image to help you feel at ease. Gradually practise this technique. Imagine yourself successfully making a start on loosening the stranglehold of anorexia nervosa next month, next week, tomorrow. Gradually, your fantasy can become reality.

By the time you finish this chapter you will be better informed about yourself and your anorexia. You will know that you are not alone in the way you feel. You will recognise that many of your thoughts and feelings belong to your illness. Recognition and acceptance that you have an illness can be a source of great comfort – until now you have been feeling grossly inadequate and weak-minded for not coping with life like others do. Now you know about the illness and what it is like, you may be wondering what the real you is really like. Perhaps you are curious to find out. Perhaps for the first time you are aware that you can be helped, that you can regain your identity and live each day without the anorexia bully bossing you about. This is indeed an exciting revelation.

- What else can you conclude?
- Are you at the stage when you want to do something about your illness?
- If so, can you confirm this out loud so that you can hear yourself say it?
- What about sharing your desire for recovery with someone else?
- Can you write this commitment down or share it with someone you trust?
- If you feel that you can't do anything about your illness yet, can you ensure that you are treading water and not getting sucked further in?
- If you feel engulfed, can you share your fears with someone you trust so that you can get extra help?
- Can you let your family or partner help more? (If you feel concerned they don't understand your illness, suggest they will find this book helpful.)
- Can you go to a day treatment centre?
- What about admission to hospital?
- Can you arrange some respite care?

Some forms of anorexia nervosa are so severe that repeated admission to hospital is necessary. Do not see this as failure. Sometimes it is necessary to go around the wheel of change many times.

Most importantly, always hold on to hope. Always! Never give up. Recovery *is* possible.

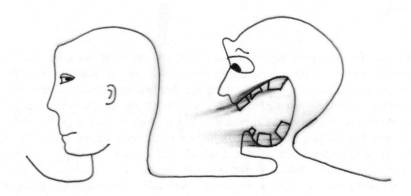

Breaking free from the anorexia bully

5   Understanding your Self

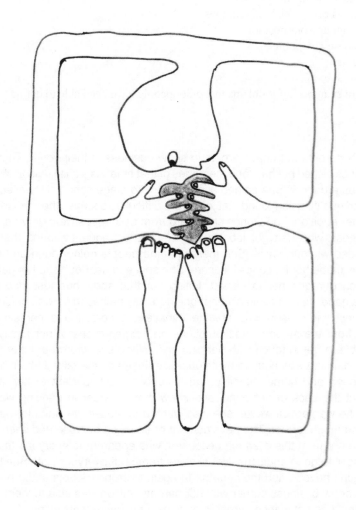

Anorexia nervosa often develops as a way of coping with a difficult situation. Your mind becomes filled with the bully thoughts that are synonymous with anorexia nervosa and food becomes a fixation. The more you think about food, the more the initial problem is suppressed and no longer causes you to feel anxious. The coping tools that the anorexia bully provides may give you an initial sense of relief as unpleasant things are shut out. However, just because you are no longer aware of the problem, doesn't mean that it is not there. It may be hidden deeply. Sometimes, the original problem is no longer an issue but you may unconsciously act as though it is still there. If you realise you have been avoiding a problem, follow these steps:

1. Clearly define the problem.
2. Brainstorm – think of solutions.
3. Weigh up your position.
4. Choose an option.
5. Review.

Here are examples of problems that other people have been able to define.

Alison

Alison's parents both had careers in show business in their youth. They had long since retired but had fond memories of that time. As a child, Alison showed talent as a dancer. She gained acceptance into stage school. However, after she had qualified she found that jobs were difficult to secure. She went to audition after audition. The stories she heard from colleagues were very depressing. Those who had got jobs in the West End frequently found that their job ended without notice. She met the same people going round and round and this made her feel quite insecure. She spoke of her doubts to her parents. They encouraged her to persist, telling her that show business had given them a good life and could give her one, too. All she had to do was persevere. In counselling, Alison was able to think about herself and her situation. Freed from the automatic assumptions and expectations of her family, she was able to get in touch with her true self. When she wrote her letter to the future, dancing was notable by its absence. Instead, she talked about having a husband and home. Stability and security were important to her. It was as if, at the back of her mind, she knew that a career in dancing was not what she wanted. However, she also wanted to please her parents who had done so much for her. The development of anorexia nervosa had seemed to release her from this dilemma because it was apparent to everyone that she was too ill to go to auditions. Her skeletal frame put everybody off. She therefore didn't have to find the courage to again raise her doubts about her proposed show business career with her parents. Alison was able to identify her problem: 'I do not want a career in dancing, only my parents want it.'

Alison listed these options for achieving a solution:

1. Continue auditioning for dancing.
2. Think of other careers.
3. Try to talk her parents round.

The first option did not appeal, so Alison focused on the next two. She was able to express her concerns about dancing and have them listened to in counselling. She was gradually able to have the space to think about a career that did not include dancing. Gradually she was able to express these doubts to her parents. At first they resisted the idea and argued against any change in plan. However, Alison by this time was feeling more confident and was able to propose that she try an alternative career for an experimental phase. Gradually her parents began to accept this idea. Alison quickly succeeded in getting a job in insurance and within months her efforts were rewarded with promotion to a higher position. With growing belief in her ability, Alison was slowly able to stand up to and fight off the sabotaging thoughts that belonged to her anorexia bully. Her parents accepted her decision and were delighted when she began to move ahead in a career that provided fulfilment.

Ruth
Ruth's parents had regularly argued during her childhood. Her dad tended to spend most of his time at the golf club or at work. At one stage her mother walked out, taking the children with her, and returned to her parents' home.

When Ruth developed anorexia nervosa, she found that her parents became close. The arguments stopped, and her father reduced his visits to the golf course so he could be at home with Ruth. To the therapist, it seemed as if Ruth was frightened of getting better because she feared her parents would revert to their previous patterns.

Ruth's anorexia was aggressive and did not allow her any insight into her illness or its trigger. She needed inpatient treatment and much therapy over a long time before she was able to discuss how her illness seemed to bring about a welcome change in the family. Acknowledging that there were family problems was difficult. Ruth was reluctant to talk, as it seemed disloyal. However, eventually she was able to identify the problem and her fear: 'My parents do not get on well. They may separate.'

Ruth's options were:

1. Continue to try to keep her parents together by her behaviour.
2. Accept that she could not be responsible for her parents, and must get on with her own life.
3. Tell her parents to separate.

Ruth chose option 2. Once Ruth saw this pattern, she began to contemplate moving out of the family home. She avoided getting drawn in to discussions about the other parent. She developed the skill of interrupting any conversation that started this way by saying: 'I do not want to be involved in discussions about your relationship unless both of you are present. If you want to talk to me about your situation, I suggest that we all meet together but I prefer not to be involved unless necessary.'

Sally

Sally's parents were both busy professionals. Her older brother, Mark, was the golden boy. He had represented his county for cricket. He had academic success and had gone on to Oxford. Sally always felt overshadowed by him. Her parents had seemed to spend all their spare time watching him play cricket or collect prizes. Once Sally developed anorexia nervosa she was aware that, for what seemed like the first time in her life, she held her parents' attention. They visited her in hospital and her mother reduced her hours at work to spend more time with her. One of Sally's fears was that if she gained weight, and looked better, then she would be forgotten again. Sally had great difficulty admitting this feeling directly. She merely hinted at it. Eventually she was able to accept and voice her problem: 'I will get ignored unless I am ill.'

Sally listed and thought about her options:

1. Remain the same.
2. Develop a circle of friends who shared a common enjoyment in life.
3. Attend navigation classes so that she could crew boats with her father.

Sally decided to try for options 2 and 3. Gradually, she developed a network of friends through her own efforts and through friends of her father.

Many people seem to develop anorexia nervosa when they are faced with distressing emotions and feel increasingly anxious because they don't know how to cope with them. The distressing emotions seem to reach an intensity that triggers the anorexia. The sufferer of course does not understand what is happening, and at first the effect of the illness seems very rewarding, as the distress appears to go immediately. Unfortunately, the distress can be retriggered very easily and becomes more intense each time it surfaces. This leads to more frantic attempts to regain control, which leads to more anorexia nervosa and a vicious circle begins. Very soon the anorexia is calling all the shots – as evidenced in behavioural and mood changes.

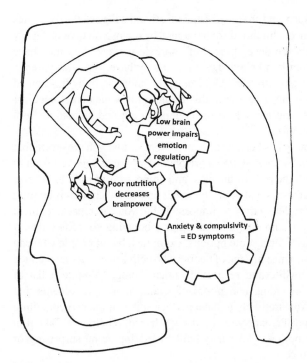

Sufferer vicious circle

When faced with strong emotions, we do know that it is important to let them run their course. They will gradually decrease and more positive emotions will return. Attempting to disrupt this process by blocking, controlling or generally trying to get rid of unpleasantness will result in kindling severe and protracted distress. This of course is recognised in common lore. A funeral wake evolved as a way of expressing feelings of loss and abandonment there and then. Some Western cultures, such as the British, however, have valued a stiff upper lip and have been puzzled by cultures that weep and wail. This is despite people in Western cultures being exposed to deeply personal events that make them sad, such as the breakdown of families. Advances in other areas of life seem to have seduced or deluded us into feeling that we have tamed nature and therefore we feel failures if things go wrong in our personal lives. But pretending everything is all right when it is not can come at a cost to your health, for the anorexia bully feeds on such attitudes.

Can you identify difficulties that you will need to face if you try to leave your anorexia bully behind? Were there problems that seemed to disappear or become bearable when your anorexia developed? Try to work your way to the bottom of the problem – working out how and why your illness started. What exactly was the difficulty or the issue? Perhaps there was more than one?

If you have been suffering anorexia nervosa for a long time, quite likely you will have layers of issues to sort. Relationship problems are likely to be at the top of your list. Separate them out into their simplest forms. Perhaps you are afraid that confronting these issues, and sharing them with others, will rock the dynamics in your family. For instance, childhood sexual abuse by a close relative or family friend sometimes triggers the development of anorexia nervosa. You may have shielded your parents from this knowledge, or you may have told your parents, who told you to 'just get on with life'. Until now, the anorexia bully has helped you cope with this pain – but it has done this by masking your unmet need for compassion and support, and has led to misunderstanding and alienation from family members who you love.

Simply, the anorexia bully has been a survival tool. Now that you are aware that this way of coping is actually keeping you a prisoner of your true self, you want to leave it behind, along with the pain of the past, and embrace your right to be free.

Clearing the backlog of issues that your illness has helped to suppress is helpful. Deleting the thoughts completely may be impossible but you can repackage them in your mind so that they are no longer affecting or sabotaging your life today. A helpful approach is to brainstorm some options. Compile a list of people who can help you deal with any lingering pain and of people who help you feel acknowledged and accepted as a worthwhile and respected human being. Compile a list of pastimes that you find rewarding and purposeful, and another of dreams that you would like to fulfil. You are likely to have perfectionistic traits and compiling these lists may not be easy. Perhaps you could ask a friend to help you. Take it in turns to add in another option. Make it playful by adding some surprising or unconventional suggestions.

Perhaps your anorexia nervosa has been such an effective smokescreen you have no idea if it is helping you avoid problems. Perhaps you can ask a friend if they can offer some insights. Maybe you will never know the trigger. Maybe there never was one. Sometimes the trigger for the development of anorexia nervosa is a major issue, such as trauma or death; other times it is a less clear and definite issue, such as teasing or feeling overlooked or rejected; other times there is no apparent trigger at all – the illness just seems to evolve. In every case, and no matter what the scenario, remember that the sufferer never chooses to have this illness. However, the sufferer must choose to recover – and this is where the love and support of trusted family, friends and recovery guides can be immeasurably helpful.

Regaining your sense of self

One of the most difficult things about anorexia nervosa is that it invades and sabotages every part of you: your thinking, your feelings and your body. It can strangle the real you like an aggressive jungle creeper smothering more delicate foliage as it soars to the sunlight. One of your first tasks is to decide what thoughts belong to you and what thoughts belong to the anorexia nervosa.

This is an enormous challenge as the physical effects of starvation lock you into vicious circles, which make it difficult to know which thoughts do reflect you and which reflect your illness. Problems and vulnerabilities produce anorexia. Lack of food – a major symptom of the illness – leads to starvation and it is nigh impossible to think clearly when your brain is starved of nutrition. The brain is plastic and is shaped by learning and experience and gram for gram requires more energy than any other organ of the body. Starvation weakens the body and spirit so that it is impossible to fight the problems. This circularity between weight loss as a consequence of the illness as well as a cause of further problems can be difficult to break.

Determining where the anorexia ends and starvation begins is complex. The Minnesota study led by Ancel Keys (1950) can help distinguish the two different aspects. The men who underwent a period of experimental weight loss described their experiences. They did not have anorexia nervosa – therefore, their experiences were due to starvation alone. Do these descriptions resonate with you?

> For a few weeks the new life was fun. I was losing weight of course, but I still had a lot of energy. Then came the day when I lost my 'will to activity'. I no longer cared to do anything that required energy and days began to drag – each day getting longer and longer and there seemed no end of starvation in sight. Six months were an eternity. But they went by. Slowly, slowly. I would compare my reflection in the mirror with that of my picture in pre-starvation days. My hair was thinner; eyes looked hollow and cheeks were only thin coverings for the bones of my face. When I tried to smile it was a grimace and I didn't feel like smiling and never laughed. My muscles were almost gone, my bones protruded (even a few seconds of sitting on a hard chair were uncomfortable) and my skin was grey and lustreless. A quarter of my original body weight had been consumed for energy during this period of deficiency. I felt as old as the aged men on my hospital ward.

How does it feel to starve? It is something like this:

> I'm hungry. I'm always hungry – not like the hunger that comes when you miss lunch, but a continual cry from the body for food. At times I can almost forget about it but there is nothing that can hold my interest for long. I wait for mealtimes. When it comes I eat slowly and make the food last as long as possible. The menu never gets monotonous even if it is the same each day or is of poor quality. It is food and all food tastes good. Even dirty crusts of bread in the street looks appetising and I envy the fat pigeons picking at them and the sight of people wasting it in restaurants is intolerable.
>
> I'm cold. In July I walk downtown on a sunny day with a shirt and sweater on to keep me warm. At night my well-fed roommate, who isn't in the experiment, sleeps on top of his sheets but I crawl under two blankets wondering why Don isn't freezing to death. My body flame is burning as low as possible to conserve precious fuel and still maintaining life processes.
>
> I'm weak. I can walk miles at my own pace to satisfy laboratory requirements, but often I trip on cracks in the sidewalks. To open a heavy door it is necessary to brace myself and push or pull with all my might. I wouldn't think of trying to throw a baseball and I couldn't jump over a 12-inch railing if I

tried. The lack of strength is a great frustration. In fact it is often a greater frustration than the hunger. I eagerly look forward to the day when I can go upstairs two at a time or maybe run to catch a streetcar.

And now I have oedema. When I wake up in the morning my face is puffy on the side I was lying on. Sometimes my ankles swell and my knees are puffy, but my oedema isn't as bad as that of several others whose flesh bulges out over their shoes in the evening. Social graces, interests, spontaneous activity and responsibility take second place to concerns of food. I lick my plate unashamedly at each meal even when guests are present. I don't like to sit near guests, for then it is necessary to entertain and talk with them. That takes too much energy and destroys some of the enjoyment that comes from my food. I no longer have the desire to help millions of starving people; rather I feel akin to them and hope that I, as well as they, will benefit from scientific re-feeding.

I am one of about three or four who still go out with girls. I fell in love with a girl during the control period but I only see her occasionally now. It's almost too much trouble to see her even if she visits me in the Lab. It requires great effort to hold her hand. Entertainment must be tame. If we see a show, the most interesting part is contained in scenes where people are eating. I couldn't laugh at the funniest picture in the world, and love scenes are completely dull.

I can talk intellectually, my mental ability has not decreased, but my will to use my ability has. So my talk is of food and past memories, or future ambitions mostly in the cooking or eating line.

This man then goes on to describe what happened when the experiment ended and they were allowed to gain weight:

That was starvation! Rehabilitation was carried on with the same food only more of it, but life came back slowly. The men were divided into four groups. I was in the lowest group and after 6 weeks of re-feeding had gained one quarter of a pound! I felt better, however, as many pounds of oedema had been replaced by healthy tissues. At the end of 6 weeks everyone was given an additional 800 calories daily. Now men in the lowest group were getting 3000 calories (about the average daily amount of the American diet) but even on this diet the average weight gain in their group twelve weeks after the end of starvation was only 7.5 pounds compared with nearly a 40 pound average loss. Now eight months after the end of starvation, I am fat and healthy although my muscles have not yet returned to their former tone. I look back to those days in July and recall my feeling of apathy.

Do you identify with any of this description? This essay is very useful as it clearly defines the effects of lack of food alone. So often in other situations of starvation, such as famines or prisoner of war camps, the effects are compounded by disease.

Spirals of starvation may entrap you

1 Physical disability

The physical complications of anorexia nervosa include weakness associated with starvation or salt or hormonal imbalance (described vividly in the earlier passage). These may heighten your sense of vulnerability or personal inadequacy, especially when you do not accept you are ill. You may view these impairments as further evidence of 'personal weakness' and intensify your efforts at achieving self-control by dieting more rigorously. A self-defeating vicious cycle is started.

2 Emotional disturbances

A brain deprived of regular nutrition cannot regulate emotions easily leading to depression and irritability. You may attempt to deal with these 'unacceptable' aspects of yourself by escalating your 'anorexic' behaviours.

Compulsive behaviours and thoughts are a feature of starvation. In conditions of famine, this has some survival advantages. Unfortunately, in anorexia nervosa this compulsive drive is often focused on anorexic behaviours and builds upon an innate tendency to follow rules. You may feel compelled to exercise more and more, or to chop your food into smaller and smaller pieces.

3 Effects on the brain. Without adequate fuel the brain has to work harder to keep up

Mental function is affected by weight loss, as was discussed by the Minnesota volunteer. Concentration, attention, memory, learning and problem solving are impaired. These effects may cloud your judgement. You will not be able to generate as many solutions when you 'brainstorm'. You may not be able to take the steps required to implement any solution. Your thinking will become even more black and white, and you will get upset more easily when your expectations are not met, or strict, self-imposed rules are broken. Your ability to use and benefit from psychological treatments requiring, as they do, new learning and flexibility in thinking, may be curtailed, reducing further the chances of recovery.

4 Effects on your social life

Your preoccupation with food (a starvation effect) limits your ability to take part in social events. You lose your interest in friendships and general topics. You lose your sense of humour. Friends become bored or feel unacknowledged and drift away. Loss of your social network heightens your feelings of alienation and distress. Unfortunately, you are tempted to deal with this with more anorexic behaviour.

5 Effect on your digestive system

You find that meals are highly distressing with mixed emotions of panic, guilt and uncomfortable physical sensations. You may have developed a conditioned aversion to some foodstuffs. Conditioning occurs when the mind learns to link an event (e.g., eating a bar of chocolate) with distressing consequences such as the image of swelling up to elephantine proportions. Even the sight of a chocolate bar can lead to panic. The longer and more completely chocolate bars are avoided, the more firmly is this new learning set down. Your mind is not given the opportunity to learn that 'death by chocolate' does not really occur. Fats are the foodstuffs now commonly linked to calamitous consequences.

You also develop physical distress in your gut. 'Bloating' or rapid fullness is due in part to a delay in the emptying of your stomach. You may become preoccupied with the thought that your stomach is swelling up like a balloon after a meal. This is because the muscles from the abdominal wall have been eaten away during the starvation and your abdominal wall therefore sags. Also, muscle from the gut wall itself is lost. This means the gut swells up with wind and fluid more than usual. The good bacteria that live in the colon are starved and depleted and irritable bowel symptoms can develop.

6 Hormones

Loss of your sex hormones from starvation can be a mixed blessing. Your sexual fantasising may stop. Your yearnings for a physical relationship vanish. This can make life very simple. Your hormones don't drive you into relationships. However, this can lead to you feeling different to everyone else; like, you are left as a bit of a misfit. It may add to feelings of being isolated and defective in some way.

7 Changes in body composition

You lose bone, brain and muscle tissue. These losses are invisible to the naked eye but can be seen by special X-rays. You may have difficulty accepting that you need to gain weight as your body is still functioning.

6 The dangers of
anorexia nervosa

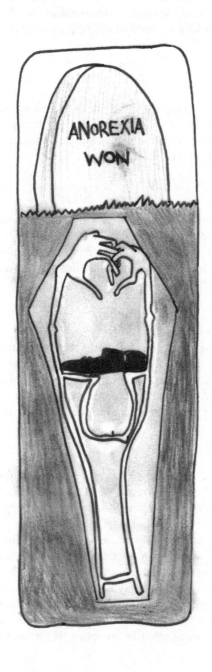

We include a description of the physical complications caused by anorexia nervosa here because an open, collaborative relationship is encouraged at all times. However, as a sufferer you may find the information distressing or too technical to understand. Feel free to skip it!

To recover from anorexia, you need to gain weight because your body is experiencing the effects of starvation. Understanding the effect that starvation has on your body, and the dangers involved will help you to appreciate the seriousness of the illness.

The risk of death

Anorexia nervosa has the highest death rate of any mental illness. It is a tragedy when a young life, or indeed a life at any age, is lost through this illness. You may have no warning. Young people with anorexia nervosa have even died in hospital where immediate help was on hand.

Susan

Susan, 19, developed anorexia two years ago. She was referred for treatment to a specialised eating disorder unit but they had no beds. She was admitted to a medical ward, but she was easily able to outsmart the busy nurses and not eat. Her weight fell and she was found dead in her bed one evening and could not be resuscitated.

Martine

Martine was a 29-year-old solicitor who struggled with her eating disorder for more than ten years. Her purging frequency became more severe under the strain of a new job. Bravely, she decided to make an appointment to see a specialist. The week before she went to clinic she suddenly collapsed. She was dead on arrival in casualty; her potassium level was very low.

The tragedy of deaths that occur in anorexia nervosa is compounded by the fact that the sufferer may be unable to understand that they are putting their life at risk. The illness bully works on convincing the sufferer that they can live on a diet of nothing.

Alternatively, the illness may distort the sufferer's thoughts with other mistaken beliefs. For example, when you have been distressed with anorexia nervosa for a long time, you may believe that death would be a relief – for you and your family. The reality is this would be a tragedy for all. Parents who lose a child never get over the death; it remains a wound to them forever. We also know that recovery from anorexia nervosa, and regaining a full and purposeful life, is achievable – at every age. Giving up must never be an option. However, the risk of death with anorexia nervosa is real, and is 16 times that of the normal population rate. The general health hazards are all the more common.

Health hazards of starvation

Effects of starvation on the body

The effects of starvation on the body include:

1. Sensitivity to cold: poor circulation results in hands and feet turning blue, mottled, swollen and subject to chilblains. Some people with anorexia nervosa have died of hypothermia.
2. Sleep disturbances: waking up early or several times in the night.
3. Weak bladder: passing water frequently throughout the day or night.
4. Excess hair growth on the body, particularly on the back, and the sides of the face.
5. Poor circulation, slow pulse, low blood pressure and fainting spells.
6. Thin bones (osteoporosis): with time, this may result in fracture leading to deformity and pain.
7. Periods stop or become very irregular. Usually, for a woman to have periods, 15 per cent of her body must be composed of fat.
8. The stomach shrinks and feels uncomfortably distended after eating even a small amount of food; stomach ulcers may be a problem that persists after recovery.
9. Gut function is slowed and constipation results.
10. The bone marrow fails. Red and white blood cells are not formed quickly enough, which results in anaemia and susceptibility to certain infections.
11. The lack of nutrition affects the liver so that it is unable to manufacture body proteins. This may result in swelling of the ankles and legs.
12. Blood cholesterol level is increased. This results from the lack of oestrogen (women before their menopause are protected from heart attacks by oestrogen) from abnormal liver function.
13. Nerves and muscles become damaged. This may make it difficult to climb stairs, the feet may drag, and extreme fatigue and tiredness supervenes.
14. In young children, growth may be stunted and puberty delayed.
15. Low glucose: this produces sensations of panic or light-headedness. If ignored, this can lead to coma and death.
16. The kidney is prone to infection and stone formation and may eventually fail.

How many of these symptoms have you experienced? Writing your own list will help you understand and acknowledge the impact of starvation on your physical health.

Common methods of weight control

Besides coping with starvation, your body has to cope with your various weight control methods. These may include the following.

Exercise

Over exercise is a common symptom. It may be used as a form of weight control or as a means to reduce anxiety or as a short-term fix for a flagging brain. However, exercise in the face of inadequate nutrition can cause long-term harm.

When weight loss is severe and energy reserves depleted, over-exercise can lead to dangerously low sugar levels. This can lead to coma and death. The wear and tear on the body can cause problems. As the bones are thin, stress fractures emerge. Muscles and joints can be damaged from increased strain.

Sometimes the need to exercise is perceived as essential to maintain a desired body shape. However over-exercise, in the context of starvation, destroys muscle and therefore shape, as your body eats up your own flesh. You cannot expect to tone up if you do not have muscle fibres.

Think of the horse in the novel *Black Beauty*. If you remember, at one stage in his life he was underfed and forced to pull a coal wagon. He collapsed and nearly died. It doesn't just happen to animals. The mortality rate among World War II Japanese prisoner of war victims increased because they were forced to work on the railways while subjected to starvation.

Vomiting and laxatives

Self-induced vomiting, laxative abuse and other extreme methods of weight control increase the health risks. In particular, there is damage to the teeth, kidney and gut. These other attempts at weight control are particularly damaging and difficult to shake off because they set up vicious circles within the brain.

Vomiting can erode the enamel on your teeth, leading to dental decay and increased sensitivity. It can lead to water and salt imbalance, which may disturb the function of the heart, brain and kidney. You may interpret feelings of weakness as due to your own lack of control, leading you to make further attempts to gain control, oblivious to the fact that such futile attempts are further endangering your health. Potassium levels can become very low and disturb the electrical activity of the heart and brain leading to heart attacks and fits. Your glands in your face may swell; this can be painful. Also, this rounding of the face will make you believe that you have become fatter, which will only make you try to control your weight more, another vicious circle. In some people, vomiting can cause tears in the stomach, which lead to life-threatening bleeding.

Vomiting does not fool the brain and body – it registers that it has no food available for metabolism and so the hunger drives are stepped up – yet another dangerous circle. This can lead to an increase in the reward attached to food and can even set up the changes of food addiction in the brain.

Like vomiting, the use of laxatives can lead to serious water and salt imbalance. This also leads to large weight fluctuations. Severe dehydration can lead to kidney failure or kidney stones. Laxatives also damage the bowel, preventing it from working normally, resulting in severe constipation and gassy distension. Straining due to use of laxatives results in piles and prolapse.

Abuse of other medications

You may have been tempted to abuse diet pills and diuretics (elimination of water tablets), obtained from pharmacies, slimming clinics or health food shops. Diuretics cause dehydration and salt imbalance and therefore damage the circulation and kidneys in a similar way to laxatives and vomiting. Diet pills taken to excess cause the body to become overactive and excitable. Sleeping may become difficult. You feel on edge, nervous and jumpy.

Your mind becomes overactive and you become suspicious and agitated. Eventually, epileptic fits may develop.

Medical investigations

The doctors helping you get over your anorexia nervosa will do a variety of medical tests and investigations to check your health.

Blood cell count

A common investigation looks at cells in the blood: red cells, white cells and platelets. If these are abnormal, it may indicate that the bone marrow is failing. This failure is due to inadequate nutrition, and reverses given an adequate food intake. The first cells to be affected are white cells. These are the cells that fight infection, either by killing or disabling germs. The normal white cell count is 4000 to 11,000 per millilitre. In anorexia nervosa the level fall may be as low as 1000 per millilitre. Obviously this has implications for the body's resistance to disease. Paradoxically, the common cold occurs less often in people who are very underweight but this is more than balanced by an increase in severe life-threatening illnesses.

The next cell to become involved is the red cell. This is the cell that carries oxygen around the body and attached to the haemoglobin molecule. A reduced haemoglobin level is known as anaemia, which leads to tiredness, breathlessness and exhaustion. In severe anorexia nervosa the level of haemoglobin can fall from the normal range of 13–15g/l, to 6g/l. The platelet level decreases in severe states of starvation. Platelets are important in repairing damage to small blood vessels, and take part in the clotting process. If platelet levels are decreased, the small blood vessels become leaky and tiny bruises form under the skin. This leads to a rash like measles. All these changes in the bone marrow and the blood cells reverse once nutrition is adequate. Calories alone are necessary in most cases. Sometimes, iron and vitamins are also needed.

BLOOD SALTS

The most common and important abnormality in blood chemistry is a low level of potassium. The normal range is 3.5–5.5mmol/l. Potassium chloride is an important salt in the body cells. The level falls if there is vomiting, diarrhoea (a result of laxatives) or use of diuretics (water tablets). In some cases the level falls as low as 2mmol/l. Potassium in the blood affects the electrical activity in cell membranes. All cells become weaker because of this. Muscles do not work well and become weak. One of the most important affected organs is the heart, as the electrical activity of the heart is responsible for making the heart beat. If the electrical activity becomes disrupted, the rhythm of the heart changes, leading to palpitations or heart attacks. The kidney also suffers, and mental confusion is a common feature.

Loss of potassium is associated with an increased bicarbonate level in the blood. The normal level of bicarbonate is 20–28mmol/l. Some patients with anorexia nervosa, complicated by vomiting or use of laxatives, have levels of bicarbonate as high as 40mmol/l. High bicarbonate level makes the blood very alkaline and this can affect the distribution of salts. One effect of this is spasm of the hands. In severe cases, epileptic fits can develop.

Laxative abuse can also lead to low levels of plasma sodium, less than 130mmol/l (the normal range is 135–145mmol/l). The cause of the low sodium is often dehydration. In some cases thirst can be absent although the mouth is dry. Low sodium can lead to weakness and faints. Muscle cramps are common. Mental apathy also occurs. Muscle twitching, convulsions and coma may arise. Other minerals in the body, such as calcium, magnesium and phosphates also can be abnormal.

What can be done? The most obvious answer is to stop doing whatever is causing the abnormality in the first place. Plan to reduce the amount of vomiting perhaps by instituting careful self-supervision. Stop taking laxatives and diuretics. This may be difficult to achieve on your own, so be brave and invite a trusted friend to be your recovery guide. Confide in this person and invite them to help you confront your self-harming thoughts.

Rapid medical replacement of the deficiencies is usually not the answer. These losses have developed slowly and the body has adapted; if rapid correction with drips of salts into the blood system occurs, it may dangerously tip the precarious balance. Similarly, it is best to replace the salts within natural foods rather than in tablet form. Foods rich in potassium include oranges, bananas and other fruits, nuts, Bovril, Marmite, chocolate and coffee.

BLOOD CHEMISTRY

Blood tests also can provide information about other systems within the body. Much of the food we eat is processed in the liver, and it is useful to look at its activity in anorexia nervosa. Severe under-nutrition damages the liver and its cells break down, releasing enzymes into the blood. Liver enzymes such as alkaline phosphatase and gamma-glutamyl transaminase may be increased. Alkaline phosphatase may be increased in younger patients during weight gain when bone turnover is increased.

Cholesterol levels are often raised above 7mmol/l, which is somewhat paradoxical given that you are likely to be on a low fat diet. The exact explanation for this is unknown although it probably relates to abnormal metabolism. If you gain weight by introducing more fats into your diet your cholesterol level will fall.

Blood glucose levels can fall in severe anorexia nervosa and this can lead to death. There have been reports of this occurring without warning, particularly in the context of excessive exercise.

BONE DENSITY

Patients with bulimia nervosa and anorexia nervosa, when tested, have been found to have reduced bone density. This can increase the risk of fracture. Some fractures, such as those of the vertebral column, cannot heal without deformity and so the effects are permanent. The degree of bone loss relates to the degree of weight loss and duration of illness. It is uncertain if full recovery of the bones is possible, particularly if the illness began before puberty. One of the major factors that influence bone density is nutrition, that is, the number of calories and how much calcium and vitamin D is available.

Bone density can be measured with special machines but, once again, the best treatment is weight gain. Eating foods that contain calcium also makes good sense. These foods include milk, cheese, nuts and pulses.

SEX AND REPRODUCTION

A major marker of an eating disorder in women is the loss of periods. This is just the tip of the iceberg as all aspects of sexual function are affected. The reproductive organs shrink in size and structure to those of a child before puberty. Without the hormonal environment associated with maturity, sexual drive also disappears. You may remember that, when you first heard about sex as a child, it seemed rather dirty and disgusting and you probably wondered: 'How can my parents do that?' When your sexual drive diminishes, sex may seem a bit like this – certainly rather boring, intrusive and unpleasant. You will no longer have sexual fantasies. You will have no urge to masturbate or have sex. If you are in a relationship, this can cause problems. You may feel obliged to please your partner and have sex. For females, reduced levels of sexual hormones will mean your vagina will be dry and sex may be painful.

What about men? What happens to your sexual function when you have anorexia nervosa? As in women, your sexuality will regress both psychologically and physically. An obvious manifestation of the physical effects is that you will no longer wake up with an erection in the morning. You will fail to get aroused by sexual stimuli that may have excited you in the past.

Tony
Tony developed anorexia nervosa when he was 22. He was not having much luck with girls. He started several relationships but lacked confidence

and none had developed into a sexual relationship. He developed anorexia nervosa after some stress at work. He noted that he no longer had erections. He interpreted this as further failure of his masculinity. He thought that he had become impotent and that his sexual life was over before it had started. He was surprised and reassured when his therapist explained that this was a side effect of starvation and that his potency would return with weight gain.

One of the men in the Ancel Keys study of starvation (see Chapter 14) described this loss of sexual appetite with starvation in this way: 'I feel no more like sex than would a sick oyster'.

Effects of starvation on the brain

As referred to in the previous chapter, starvation also affects the brain and behaviour and these effects include:

1. Emotion regulation is impaired. Mood is lowered and depression results in pessimism, hopelessness and inability to find pleasure in life.
2. The mind becomes preoccupied with food and there is often a strong urge to overeat. This craving, 'fed' by a disrupted pattern of eating, can lead to binge eating.
3. The ability and interest in forming relationships is diminished. Friendships are lost. There is a feeling of being isolated from others, and of a yearning to be alone.
4. Concentration is poor. Working to full capacity is not possible.
5. Minor problems appear insurmountable.
6. Complex thought is impaired. Holding several threads of thought in place at once is difficult.

Many authors have written about the effects of starvation, albeit usually not self-imposed (see reading list on page 169).

Permanent damage

When physical complications are discussed, this question always arises: 'What will be the long-term problems?' Answering with confidence is difficult, as relatively few studies have followed the health of sufferers over time. Most of the physical problems do reverse with weight gain, or if the weight control practices stop. Other factors include the duration of illness and the stage of life at which the illness arose. For example, there may be a critical time during which puberty can take place. If the illness strikes before all the stages of puberty have been attained and recovery is delayed, there may be irreversible failure to achieve growth in stature, peak bone density and secondary sexual development.

The reproductive system is obviously affected and many people are concerned about the long-term effects. Probably, if there is full recovery, all will return to normal, although it may take longer than normal to conceive. In some cases, hormonal treatment may be necessary. The difficulty is that between one-third and one-half of all sufferers may have residual problems and remain under their optimal weight. They are likely to experience problems such as poor fertility, an increase in the rate of miscarriages and complications during pregnancy.

We do not know to what extent bone density recovers. There is some evidence that, with a short illness, the bones can regain their strength and thickness. Repairs may take a long time and some will take longer than others. Recovery may be incomplete. If bones remain thin, the risk of fracture is increased. Bones in the spinal column may be crushed because they are thin and fragile and the subsequent loss of height and spinal curvature are irrecoverable. This may lead to chronic pain.

The long-term effects on the heart and circulation are also unknown. In the general population, 'yo-yo' dieting is associated with an increased risk of cardiovascular disease and death. Patients on very low fat diets often have raised levels of cholesterol.

After recovery, gut problems can remain. Heartburn and stomach ulcers are more common. The bowel can become 'irritable' with frequent diarrhoea or severe constipation.

Weight control measures that alter salt and water balance can lead to permanent kidney damage. As the kidneys have a lot of reserve function, this may not become apparent unless they are put under further stress.

If the brain learns a pattern of binge eating and food addiction, the 'unlearning' process can take a while. Ideally you are wise to do all you can to prevent this situation happening by eating a mixed nutritionally balanced diet at regular intervals and not taking up behaviours that try to trick the brain by 'chewing and spitting' or vomiting.

Overview

Anorexia nervosa is a potentially life-threatening illness. The long list of complications may cause you to feel worried and frightened, or even angry and guilty that your health is at such risk. However, information about these serious and severe physical complications may inspire and improve your motivation to aim for recovery. Rather than despairing and thinking that the future seems more hopeless, feel confident that you can regain both your true sense of self and your physical health. The aim of this book is to provide the facts you need. Treatment, in the absence of weight gain, has little impact on the disorder or your health. No matter how uncomfortable and difficult, remember that a primary goal is to improve nutrition.

7 Body composition and nutrition

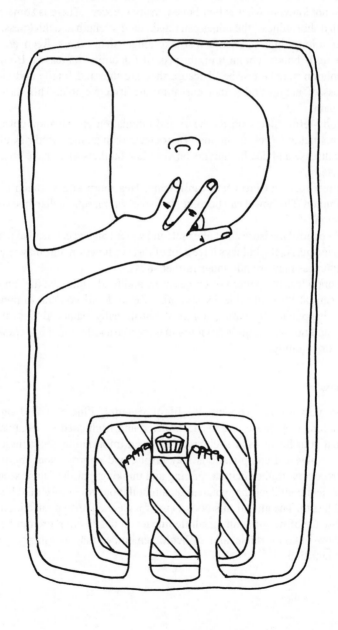

Weight control

What is a reasonable weight?

Assessment of a healthy weight must take height into account. Medically, one of the best and simplest methods of doing this is to calculate the body mass index (BMI). The BMI is weight in kilograms divided by the height in metres squared. The healthy BMI range is 20–25. If we define health as lowest mortality, then we find that the healthy range increases with age. The lowest mortality is at BMI $19.5kg/m^2$ for women at age 20 and $27.3kg/m^2$ at age 60.

Table 7.1 shows the normal range of BMI, which is between 20 and $25kg/m^2$. The World Health Organisation (1990) sets a BMI of $17.5kg/m^2$ as the threshold for anorexia nervosa. A BMI of $13.5kg/m^2$ is a critical level of weight loss at which admission to hospital should be considered.

You can see from the table that a wide range of weights is normal. At least half of the population, by definition, is in the top half of the range. Interestingly, the fittest people are often in the top half of the range because muscle tissue is quite dense; it is much denser and heavier than fat, for example. Genetic make-up is a major variable affecting body weight and composition. Some people are born with a bigger and stronger skeletal frame and the muscles to go with it.

Table 7.1 Normal, anorexic and dangerous weights

Height m (ft)	1.52m (5'0")	1.57m (5'2")	1.63m (5'4")	1.68m (5'6")	1.73m (5'8")
Normal range BMI 20–25	45–56kg 46–58kg	48–60kg 49–62kg	51–64kg 53–66kg	54–68kg 56–71kg	58–72kg 60–75kg
Anorexia Nervosa BMI < 17.5	40kg	43kg	47kg	49kg	52kg
Medical danger BMI < 13.5	31kg	33kg	36kg	38kg	40kg

Effect of bodily systems

Bodily systems are designed to maintain a steady internal state. These rules apply to body composition and weight. Weight loss leads to powerful counterbalancing forces to restore body mass. However, the control of body weight is more complex than, say, the control of blood oxygen level, in that it involves a motivational state, appetite and food-seeking behaviour. Also the system is not symmetrical. The mechanisms to prevent weight loss are more powerful than those which prevent weight gain. This can be understood in terms of the threats to human life in the past when starvation was more common.

Food requirements

In most people, appetite is tightly linked to energy use, which is reflected in their body's metabolic rate. In anorexia nervosa, metabolic rate is slowed so less energy is expended at rest. This leads to coldness and fatigue. As soon as food intake is reduced, a clampdown on energy expenditure occurs to minimise the amount of weight loss. In anorexia nervosa, the metabolic rate is increased after recovery, perhaps above normal levels. The mechanism for this is unknown. Perhaps it represents a constitutional tendency to burn off energy more quickly, or it may be that after an episode of anorexia nervosa there is a long period when metabolism is increased to repair the damage caused by the period of starvation.

Hormonal changes also affect metabolism. Women in the second half of their menstrual cycles are metabolically more active, as their bodies prepare for egg implantation. One sign of increased metabolism is the increase in body temperature seen after ovulation.

A person's energy needs can be calculated, although this does not take into account the genetic and hormonal factors just discussed, but rather provides an estimate of average metabolism. The World Health Organisation's standard equations (e.g., WHO, 1985) give a reasonably accurate estimate of maintenance energy requirements in calories per day (see Appendix):

> To gain weight in the face of this basal requirement, 500 extra calories per day are needed to produce a predictable weight gain of 0.5kg per week. The basal metabolic rate needs to be recalculated at various intervals to account for the increase in weight, metabolism, and activity level. Once weight gain has started the basal requirements increase.

Remember this fact when you worry about initially gaining weight after only a small increase in your food.

It is not just the amount eaten that is critical but also the pattern of eating. Regular small meals should be eaten throughout the day. Human physiology has evolved to this style. We are not like the big cats, which can gorge once daily or less. We are more like vegetarian mammals, which eat small amounts throughout the day. Eating small, frequent meals increases metabolic rate. This means you have to eat more to keep pace, but this pattern is associated with a much better metabolic profile.

- Long gaps between meals signal the body to conserve energy and so any food will be selectively deposited as fat in the expectation of famine. As the balance between fat and lean is disturbed, weight may increase to redress the balance.
- Eating at night has the same effect. At this time the body's hormonal profile promotes storage, in preparation for the fast during sleep.

The pattern of eating can become totally disrupted.

Sharon

I developed anorexia nervosa at the age of 13. I had partially recovered but my BMI remained below 17.5. I knew that I needed to gain weight, but couldn't manage to eat regular meals. My sleep pattern became disrupted. I would waken three or four times in the night and be driven to get up and eat, otherwise I couldn't get back to sleep. I felt very out of control, eating at night, and my family complained that I disturbed their sleep. I had difficulty getting up in the morning to go to work, and avoided breakfast because I felt so guilty about eating during the night.

Sharon's treatment involved gradually shifting her eating pattern. She arranged to start work in the middle of the day to provide at least some structure in her life. She agreed to eat a meal with her mother before setting out for work. Gradually, she set the alarm earlier each morning, introduced breakfast within an hour of getting up and ate another meal before going to work. During this time her sleep remained disrupted. So she began taking novels to bed and did not plan to sleep immediately, instead reading her latest book and focusing on feeling snug, warm and comfortable. In this way, Sharon gradually reduced the amount she ate at night. Eventually, if she woke at night she did not have to eat before she could fall back to sleep. This weight restoration took more than a year, but eventually Sharon was able to sleep throughout the night.

When the clamp on diet is lifted

Weight

The first stage of recovery is very difficult. The pattern of weight gain may not appear to be in step with the changed eating pattern. Weight fluctuations can be large, as glycogen stores in the liver are replenished and packed with water. This rapid rate of weight gain stops and later more food will be needed to continue to gain weight.

Weight gain after severe starvation usually leads to an increase in fluid in association with restoration of glycogen stores. In some cases up to 15kg of water accumulates. Vomiting, laxatives or diuretics increase the risk of this happening. One to three months may be needed for the body to re-establish a normal fluid balance. During this time fluid will collect around the eyes overnight and around the ankles at the end of the day. The sensation of bloating and the obvious swelling may act to vindicate your blackest fantasies. Your biggest fear – uncontrollable weight gain and a visibly larger body – appears to be happening.

The pattern of fat distribution during weight gain may upset you. You may be sensitive about your stomach becoming bigger. But don't despair because most of this distension is just an increase of wind and fluid in the sluggish gut.

The digestive system

The digestive system shrinks and slows down if food is limited. The gut has to adapt gradually to being stretched and fed again. During this early phase, bloating and abdominal discomfort are common. This is because stomach emptying is slowed down. Stretching and reconditioning of muscle fibres within the gut walls causes some discomfort. This may take several months to subside. Some people become very aware of their stomach distending, particularly after meals. During this early stage you may want to avoid too much roughage, especially the type with insoluble fibre, such as bran, as this may be harder to digest.

Starting to eat

Starting to eat again is difficult. The anorexic bully shouts and screams. Anxiety levels increase to such a high level that keeping recovery in mind is difficult. Like any new activity, the best way to start is to gradually get in training rather than dive in at the deep end. In hospital, severely underweight patients start off on a sloppy, old-fashioned invalid-type diet with scrambled eggs, nutritious soups and milky puddings. The next step is half portions of 'normal' food comprising approximately 1250kcal. Again, the food is divided into three meals and three snacks. As weight is gained, a gradual increase in the amount eaten is necessary to maintain a steady increase in weight. The risk of developing bulimia is much lower on a weight-gaining regime like this. Food addiction/ bulimia can arise if the brain is exposed to 'surprises'; for example, if prolonged fasting is interrupted by a sudden rush of glucose/fat from a binge on highly palatable foods. Another 'surprise' occurs if the body prepares to metabolise food seen and tasted but which does not arrive in the blood because of spitting and vomiting.

Developing strategies to cope with the distress you may experience when you begin to eat again is helpful. Some sufferers watch television or listen to the radio during meals; others eat with family members or close friends, read a favourite classic work of literature – carrying the story line and discussion from meal to meal – solve a puzzle or read something 'light' such as a detective story. Here are examples which have worked for others.

Alex

I started to eat after my illness caused me to starve myself for eight years. During the first few weeks I had very painful stomach pains, cramps, bloating and wind. I felt sick, constantly. Nevertheless, I really wanted to regain my life and was determined to persist and succeed. One of the scariest times was when I started to feel hungry. I feared I would start to eat and never be able to stop. I imagined my stomach wall would surely burst. Trusted friends agreed to help keep me on track at times like this when I became demoralised and frightened. They helped me stick to the three meals and three snacks a day plan no matter what, and sure enough, I eventually found that the fear of over-eating was merely another phase. I got through it.

Sally

I began a silent argument with myself whenever I felt guilty after eating. I visualised talking to the anorexia saboteur in my mind: 'I know it's only you that is making me feel guilty. You are frightened that you are losing your grip on me and you are kicking up a fuss. You are right. I am determined to ignore you. I am determined to be free. I now recognise you for what you are – a bully – and am deleting all the tormenting thoughts that belong to you. In this way, I can shut out your seductive voice and focus on regaining the real me.' Sometimes she even exchanged chairs to act out this conversation.

Robert

I made sure that I always ate with a friend. When the anorexia bully shouted and screamed in my mind, I tried hard to ignore it and concentrate on what my friend was saying. I encouraged him to talk about things that had amused me before the illness had developed. We came up with a secret code so that I could indicate to him when I was feeling tense and could feel an anorexia trigger coming on. My friend would respond quickly to defuse the trigger and divert my attention to something light-hearted, pleasant and real in the here and now.

Fiona

The use of imagery helped me to distract myself from anorexia's bossy thoughts. I imagined myself walking away from this bully. I followed this image, constructing a daydream in which I was taking part in an exciting adventure. I took the image and the story from one meal to the next. Eventually I really did leave the anorexia bully behind and life really did become an exciting adventure.

The reading list on page 168 may help you put issues of nutrition and weight and shape into perspective. Some of the books are novels.

8 Digging deeper

Understanding personality patterns

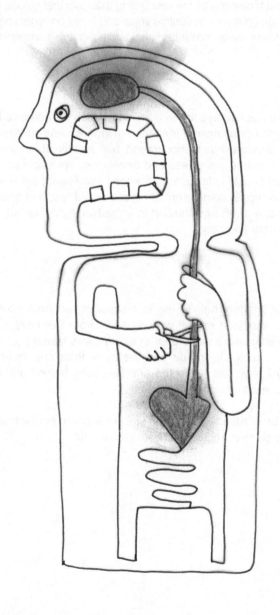

Certain personality traits may have increased your vulnerability to develop anorexia nervosa. We each have underlying patterns of thinking, feeling and behaving that comprise our personality. Some patterns are genetic; some are formed when we are in the womb; and some are shaped by other developmental influences.

Understanding our development, and how we learn to understand the world and, more importantly, the people in it, is a helpful step in overcoming anorexia. The developing brain of a child observes events and actions and notes consequences in others and themselves. These are stored as circuits in memory and have been called 'schemata'. The same child may experience the world very differently if the characteristics of their parents differ. For example, a child with an anxious disposition raised by parents with the same characteristics is likely to experience over-protectiveness. The child will strongly believe that the world is a frightening place because of their parents looking after their every need, and they will feel extremely vulnerable.

However, the same child brought up by parents who are bold and do not appear to see dangers may feel confused. In this instance, the child's own reactions are not endorsed. They may have difficulty knowing whether they can trust their feelings. This may lead them to feel worthless, guilty and insecure because their view of the world does not match that of their parents. When the main people in their life do not validate their reactions to experiences, they build up somewhat confused schemata.

This adjustment between the temperament of the child and that of the family and peers shifts when the child leaves home, or if the family situation alters. The patterns of behaviour experienced in the family no longer hold true. This discrepancy between the actual and the expected pattern can cause trouble. Old patterns of behaviour can become self-defeating, or lead to harm in relationships with others. Despite this, because they are deeply entrenched and are central to the sense of self, they are very difficult to change.

Schemata that contain pervasive themes regarding yourself and your relationship with others, and that have developed during childhood but are dysfunctional in some way, have been called 'early maladaptive schemata'. Think of these memory circuits as having buttons, which certain situations can trigger and put you into a type of automatic pilot mode.

When you have these early maladaptive schemata, you can react in different ways. You can go on feeling, acting and behaving as if they were true, or you can over-compensate and act in an opposite way. For example, those who feel they need to be obedient and in control in most situations may be officious, domineering and authoritarian in other circumstances, perhaps with their dog! Other people go out of their way to avoid triggering their schema as it leads to unpleasant emotions. For example, someone who feels inferior or defective will strive to be perfect to avoid awakening the 'failure/not-coming-up-to-scratch schema'.

A group of personality features or schemata are characteristic of anorexia nervosa. These include perfectionism, the need for self-discipline or control, the need to please others and a sense of inner defectiveness.

Insecure attachment

Many behaviour patterns seen in anorexia nervosa reflect an underlying assumption that all love is conditional, that love has to be bought and deserved by effort. Love seems not freely given but conditional. Part of the self appears to be a harsh, omnipresent authority figure that expects and demands high standards of behaviour, achievement and appearance. Anxiety grows in response to the fear that failure to attain these standards will lead to rejection.

This type of schema or thinking pattern can cause problems when you enter new relationships in adult life. This is because you have learnt that a balance of care and affection, need and support is not possible. You may be supportive for others, but will have difficulty accepting help and care from them. This may not be a problem in more superficial relationships where people are happy to use your nurturing gifts without giving anything back. You may even be in a job where this is necessary, such as nursing. But it will cause problems in deeper relationships with equals. Your inability to share your own needs may appear as distancing or as lack of trust. The lack of reciprocity in the relationship will lead to your partner feeling uncomfortable. The lack of balance, and of give and take, will make them feel uneasy, selfish or even abusive.

Was there a time in childhood when you felt your needs for attention, care and love were too much to bear and nobody was listening? Was it impossible for you to show any negative emotions as a child without being criticised? Were feelings of hurt, loss, distress and jealousy dismissed as unacceptable? Can you discuss this with your recovery guide? If confronted now, with yourself as a child, would your needs seem at all unreasonable? Most likely, they will seem most reasonable. Now, as an adult, can you see why your parents were unable to give you what you needed? Can you understand why they had difficulty tolerating distress in others? Does this insight help you accept that this happened to you then, but does not have to keep happening, and affecting your life, now?

Penny

I was the older of two children. Our father left home when I was six years of age. Our mother had to go out to work. We were left in the care of a child minder who seemed to take a dislike to me. She punished me physically and verbally and forced me to do jobs and be late for school. I always liked to be at school on time and felt I was letting the teacher down. The child minder's own children and my brother appeared to escape her animosity. One of the worst aspects was the unpredictability of the child minder's moods and attacks. I never knew when she would snap at me and did not understand why she did so. I kept quiet about all of this. I did not dare tell Mum, as I knew that she had to go out to work to make ends meet. I felt that Mum had enough difficulties in her life and I didn't want to add to these by sharing my concerns.

Penny developed anorexia nervosa in her teenage years. She was able to avoid hospitalisation and was even able to keep relationships going, maintaining a bright happy facade. However, when relationships started to become more serious she ran into problems. On two occasions, her partners became uneasy about commitment. In therapy, Penny was able to recognise how difficult it was for her to accept and receive help. She would cancel one out of three sessions. In some ways, she was the perfect patient and would do her homework diligently. However, she had difficulty acting on any of the solutions that were reached in the therapy sessions. A breakthrough occurred when Penny started to keep a diary of the times that she avoided discussing or even thinking of her own needs or deliberately suppressing them. She began to try to let her husband help. For example, she let him prepare her breakfast each day and sat down to eat it with him. Over time, their relationship gradually improved.

Perfectionism

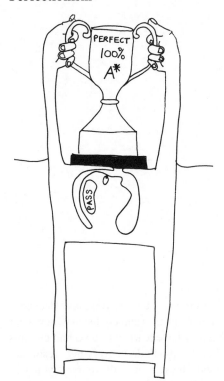

Perfectionism

Insecurity in relationships, with your self and with others, can lead to coping by grasping at markers of acceptability. These markers may include sensitivity to culturally endorsed values (thinness, diet), cleanliness or academic success. A constant striving for perfection can follow, especially if you have a personality style that values detail and order and abides by rules.

Self-control and discipline

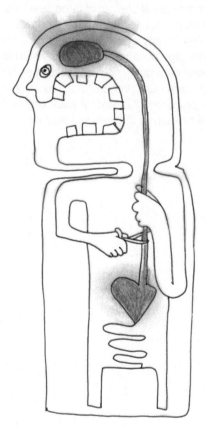

Self-control and discipline

If you have strengths in self-control and discipline – that is, you make decisions with your head rather than your heart – you may dismiss and not listen to how your body signals your feelings and needs. You may have learned to bind and gag this aspect of yourself, perhaps because you fear that it will drain everyone's resources or you will make a mistake. If you exclude these voices of yourself you will become like a robot following rigid rules and routines.

How do the illustrations in this chapter make you feel? What thoughts do you have when you see these images? Note them down.

This rigid pattern of behaviour stunts brain growth and inhibits learning and creativity. Training yourself in flexibility is important as this is an essential life skill, which promotes wisdom and maturity.

An eye for detail

People with anorexia nervosa are often highly gifted in finding detail. This skill can be an asset in some forms of academic work (such as science, law and accounting), but if it outweighs the ability to grip the gist, it can be a hindrance. Starvation impairs the brain's ability to connect and see the bigger picture, so the focus on detail and tunnel vision becomes stronger.

Training your brain to step into other people's perspectives and take the long view is an essential part of recovery and restoration to a fulfilled life.

Stop start

Alternatively there can be black-and-white, extreme behaviours that may underpin the development of binge eating. The Henry Wadsworth Longfellow poem *There was a Little Girl* describes a young girl who could be very, very good or bad and very horrid, indicating that, even as young children, girls are portrayed in extreme ways. Later, the Madonna/Whore split comes into play.

Do you recognise any of these features in yourself? Do you have an inner voice that is quick to chastise and slow to praise? Look at these drawings.

There was a little girl

Teacher

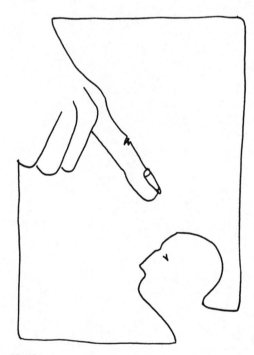

Headmaster

Do you identify with any of the messages in these drawings? Write a list of the thoughts they arouse within you. Do they remind you of similar experiences? If so, try to write down a description of these. Do the images relate to scenes from your childhood? Can you discuss this with your recovery guide? Does your guide see any perfectionistic traits in you? With their help perhaps you can notice when this part of you emerges, and what triggers it into action.

Keep a diary of how often these thoughts are coming. What terror is it that keeps these tormenting thoughts alive and kicking? Do you really believe that you would be rejected, unloved and abandoned unless you meet the high standards you feel compelled to meet? Or is it more a fear of being criticised or humiliated if you get things wrong? Think back to your childhood. Do you have a memory of something like this happening as a child? Did it actually happen or was it implied? Children can be very sensitive to these messages and have no way of judging them against a different standard. Children have a strong need for love and attention so they quickly learn the rules for this to happen. When these schemata or memory circuits are implanted in your mind, much effort is required to remove them but, with help, you can do it.

Discuss with your recovery guide the terrors you are trying to avoid. What critical judge are you trying to appease? If a friend, or even your child, believed they must live by the same rules, what would you tell them? Can everybody win every competition? How many people can be above average? Is it possible that your drive for perfectionism may lead to a continuous demand to be competitive? Others may find this irritating or depressing. They may find that living with such high standards too difficult, or they may start to feel jealous or envious of your success. They may resent being shown up as lazy or messy. By having such high standards you may set yourself up to fail or to become exhausted. Can you take up less competitive activities? This might include playing with children or doing voluntary work for the disabled.

Try to see yourself more realistically. Accept the rhythm – the ups and downs – of life. Know that if something is making you unhappy, this feeling will pass. Nothing stays the same. Things will get better. Think about other ways of feeling good, rather than relying on a structure of power and achievement. Try reading books on feminist theories, which question this male-dominated model.

We all are mixtures of good and bad, and we all have times when we are full of energy and other times when we need to draw in on ourselves. Try to pay attention to the positive aspects of yourself and forgive yourself for your flaws. Construct a list of your positive qualities. If this is challenging, invite your recovery guide to help. You will be surprised to find that you have a lot going for you.

Set up little experiments for yourself to test your perfectionistic rules of living. Try to lower your standards in one area of your life. Perhaps leave the dishes on the sink when you go to bed, or leave your clothes on the floor, or leave the office on time instead of working behind for an hour or two. Observe what happens. You are likely to find that your world does not fall in and, better still, that you are starting to feel less pressured and less anxious. You are giving your brain a chance to grow more.

Susie

> I was aged 24 when I began my recovery journey from anorexia nervosa. I had developed the illness at the age of 15. I had one period of inpatient treatment but failed to gain weight and quickly relapsed. My perfectionism took the form of keeping the home clean and tidy. I was the youngest in the family with three older brothers. My father was somewhat of a perfectionist himself and worked long hours to ensure that his standards were maintained. He had difficulty relaxing at home and would tend to go off to the pub to play darts. I felt that he gave me little attention, apart from my school reports. He was pleased when I achieved top marks and encouraged me to persist and to obtain the high level of education that he had never enjoyed. I interpreted this as meriting Dad's attention only if I attained high standards. Otherwise I did not feel worthy.

In therapy, Susie kept a diary of how often this approval-seeking behaviour was triggered in her adult life. She set herself several small experiments in which she gradually tried to decrease her cleaning behaviour. Progress was very slow because she still had strong urges to aim for high standards and her schemata were firmly entrenched. One day, however, she was suddenly able to step outside her narrow and rigid patterns of behaviour. She was able to be more objective and view her habits like an outsider. She told her therapist how her urge to clean was so strong that, when a family member was eating a snack while watching television, she would be beside them ready to sweep up each fallen crumb. Susie began to giggle as she saw the funny side of it. Once this breakthrough occurred, she quickly developed the skill of recognising and defusing the perfectionist trigger before it went off, by conjuring up that amusing image.

Emotional intelligence

If strong in-built rules and detail control your life, you may need to lift this tight control to let your emotional intelligence develop.

One of the first steps is to understand what emotions are and how they can affect you. Some of these feelings will be painful and distressing. You may have been able to put them aside or ignore them by starving but all you have done is put them on hold rather than deal with them effectively. You cannot avoid the work that needs to be done to process emotions. For example, if you have lost someone who was important to you, going through the pain and difficulty of grieving is essential for healing to take place. If you attempt to short-circuit your grief, it will only pop up again later.

Painful and distressing emotions are part of life. They cannot be banished. Although they can feel overwhelming, you can develop strategies to cope with them. You will be able to tolerate them. They are not disgusting or sinful.

Recovery from anorexia nervosa requires you to learn new skills, especially those related to emotion regulation. You need to accept and know that you don't have to try to avoid or suppress negative emotions in order to cope. You will be able to master unpleasant emotions with techniques such as support from others and self-soothing and acceptance. Issues that you may want to deal with in counselling, or with your friend or recovery guide, include:

1. Understanding the emotions you experience.

    a) Identify the emotions.
    b) Understand these emotions and what they do, and mean, to you.

2. Reducing your emotional vulnerability and imbalance.

    a) Decrease negative vulnerability – recognise that you are a glass half full person and are highly attuned to the negative, whereas other people look on the brighter side of life.
    b) Increase positive emotions (train your attention to cherish acts of kindness and to register the beauty of small things).

3. Decreasing emotional suffering.

    a) Let go of painful emotions through mindfulness and acceptance.
    b) Share your pain (and joy) with others. We are social animals and our brains are wired up to thrive in groups.

A good way to approach this is to think of ways of soothing your five senses (it is all right to exclude the sense of taste!). Examples include:

*   *Vision*: buy a flower, go to an art gallery, or light a candle.
*   *Hearing*: listen to music; sing a favourite song.
*   *Smell*: use your favourite perfume or try some new scents in a shop. Use some techniques of aromatherapy or buy a bunch of your favourite flowers.
*   *Touch*: take a bubble bath (with lots of bubbles), cuddle a pet, have a massage, soak your feet.
*   *Taste*: you may even be able to enjoy this one some time soon!

Competition and/or pleasing behaviour

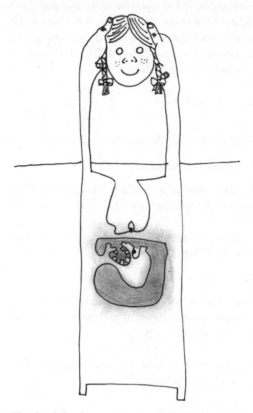

Pleasing behaviour

Another common schema in anorexia nervosa leads sufferers to believe and act as if they are worthless or defective. To compensate for and hide this inner badness and source of shame, there is a strong drive to please. Sufferers can behave like doormats, letting others tread on them. In some cases, the feeling of worthlessness in relationship to others can alternate with its opposite, a need to compete. This may cause you to feel contemptuous of others who spend much energy and time on eating.

Finding the balance between feeling looked down on and trampled underfoot, and looking down on others, is a challenge.

Thinking back to your childhood, were there times when you felt a strong drive to please? Did your position in the family mean that you were noticed only if you joined up with someone else?

If you suppress your own needs and wishes to please others you are likely to end up furiously angry. Even if you are an Oscar-winning actor, you will be unable to hide this resentment forever. Others can feel deeply disconcerted when a seemingly compliant and easy-going person becomes transformed into a 'vitriolic harridan'. If you always say 'yes', others have difficulty seeing and respecting you as a person. Your behaviour is like that of a robot – but there is a big difference: robots don't have feelings, and you do.

Hannah

I was the youngest in a family of three. I followed my older sister to boarding school. My sister had been a star pupil and became head girl. I could not compete so turned away from academic pursuits and instead aimed to be liked by my school friends. I became the class joker. I could always be relied on for creating mischief, and earned the title of most misbehaved student in the class. I had difficulty in settling in to any career or training after school. Within a year I accidentally became pregnant. I mean, I had not thought that I would need any contraception. This was a bit of a wake up call. I arranged a termination and told only two close friends. I sure did not want to tell my parents – they would have flipped – and the next day when I returned home I had to join in a game of social tennis with family and friends as if nothing had happened. My anorexia developed after a trip to New Zealand with a girlfriend. On my return to London this same girlfriend became involved in a relationship and cut me out of her life. This was one of the stressful events that preceded my illness.

A major issue in Hannah's therapy was the recognition of her tendency to please others, rather than thinking what she would like for herself. She started to keep a diary of when these events occurred. In sessions she practised role playing some of the scenarios in a more assertive manner. Little by little she was able to change her interactions with friends. However, progress was slow and there was the tendency to relapse. For example, when her therapy stopped and she went away to university, she became involved in a relationship with a man who was highly regarded in her set as 'cool', but who demeaned and walked all over her. Hannah's eating deteriorated and she lost weight. However, by the time she returned for a follow-up therapy session she was able to recognise what had happened, accepted that the relationship was destructive for her health and ended it.

One of the first steps in dealing with the pleasing 'trap' is to identify and express your own preferences and natural inclinations. Women have lived in a male-dominated environment for many years. They have adapted to this powerless position by behaving passively, or obtaining what they want by indirect 'manipulative' ways. Sometimes women have difficulty acknowledging their preferences or what they really want.

The learning of skills can help overcome a lack of confidence in knowing when and how to be assertive. You need to learn how to balance priorities versus demands, and 'wants' versus 'shoulds'. Many women see assertiveness as an aggressive response, or any expression of their own needs as selfishness. However, there is a wide, open space of middle ground between passivity and aggression, and between selflessness and selfishness. You can develop an appropriate degree of assertion and self-nurturance. You need to work on what goals are appropriate for you. Often, this can be complex and requires you to balance your needs with the needs of others and your own moral principles. You will need to learn to give and take and use negotiation skills.

Inner defectiveness

An underlying cause behind the need to please and to be perfect may be the inner conviction that somehow one is defective: 'No one would like me if they knew the real me' or 'When people like me, I feel I am fooling them and they must surely soon realise that I am fake'. Do you identify with these types of thoughts?

Have there been times when people have expressed their disgust or criticism of you, or said things that made you feel undermined, inadequate and worthless? Were there times when this happened as a child?

Were there times when people said things that made you feel ashamed, criticised or humiliated? Would you be able to discuss some of these memories and images with your recovery guide? Does your recovery guide think it appropriate that you were treated in this way as a child? What would your guide say if they saw someone talking like this to their child? Did your guide get criticised in a similar way when they were young?

These personality features or schemata are contributing factors that 'feed' the anorexic behaviour. Intercepting and attending to these factors in a healthy way is vital because the anorexia trigger is hard to stop once it goes off. The need to achieve weight loss can quickly tap into the perfectionist schema, which leads to the desire for having the ideal shape to fit with society's expectations. The need to control one's own impulses and drives becomes transformed into the need to control hunger. Low self-esteem/inner defectiveness can be masked if your outer shell is acceptable to society. The extreme effect of some of these positions makes the opposite appear terrifying and so any shift becomes difficult.

9   Links in generations

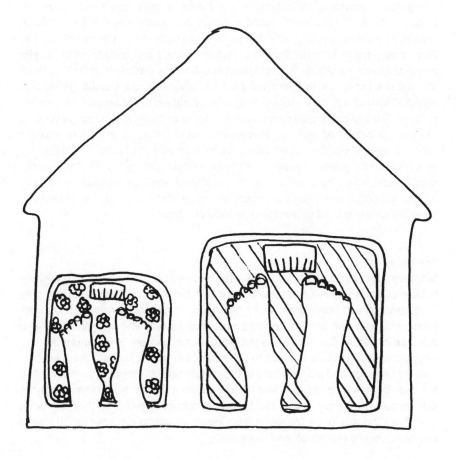

A genetic vulnerability is involved in the development of anorexia nervosa. The risk is greatest for female relatives and the incidence is higher in Western culture. The culture or environment does not cause eating disorders but it 'feeds' their triggers or symptoms through the promotion of a slim and fit body physique – the message being that only people who are slim and fit are desirable and worthy. The combination of genetic and environmental factors means it is not uncommon for two sisters to have an eating disorder. In one out of 14 families, another family member will be affected. This causes additional difficulties.

If the mother has an eating disorder, mealtimes are more complex. Often, the mother may never have eaten with the family or, if she has, she has always eaten different meals. Perhaps she sits down to a plate piled high with steamed yellow and green vegetables, while serving her family a more nutritional meal that includes slices of roast beef, baked potatoes and gravy. Or she fusses about, ensuring everyone is eating well, but picks on a sparrow-sized meal herself. The mother may try to hide her behaviour but her family and friends notice it. Her preoccupation with shape, weight, fitness and diet may directly transfer to a child. We saw in Chapter 1 how Clare had a mother who, although she did not have an eating disorder, set high standards for her daughter's appearance and eating patterns. We can easily understand how this focus on body image may develop in our present culture of thinness. Parents of a fat child are often criticised as not caring enough about their child. However, as indicated in Chapter 2, weight may be under strong genetic control, with some people gaining weight more easily than others. Also, there are phases in childhood and development, especially around puberty, when a certain amount of 'puppy fat' is normal. The increase in fat in females is related to the ability to have children.

Margaret
Margaret, an Anglo-Indian, was adopted at the age of one year into a white middle-class family in which there were two older sons. A younger boy was also adopted two years later. From the age of nine, Margaret did not under-stand why, but her mother became preoccupied with the weight of her two adopted children. She had a weight chart in the kitchen. She served the two adopted children different meals to the rest of the family, forbade them to have second helpings and put little food in their lunch packs. Margaret compensated for this by stealing money from her mother's purse and buying snacks and sweets away from home. Her friends at school also shared their food with her. From the age of 14 Margaret developed an eating disorder which varied between severe restriction and bingeing.

In other cases where an eating disorder develops, the mother may try to prevent her own attitudes to shape and weight from affecting her child and yet may be horrified to notice her daughter developing anorexic behaviours.

Rachel

Rachel's mother developed anorexia nervosa before her marriage. She recovered and gave birth to Rachel, but suffered a relapse shortly afterwards. Following treatment for infertility, she had twins several years later. Her anorexia nervosa persisted but was not medically severe and she never received treatment.

Rachel began to develop anorexia nervosa at the age of 13 after being bullied at school and among her friends via social messaging. Her mother thought that the family should eat together but mealtimes became more and more stressful. Rachel always felt that her mother was putting too much food on her plate. She sensed that there was competition and rivalry between them. She feared that her mother wanted to make her fat. However, Rachel's mother was very aware of how anorexia had nearly destroyed her own life. She likened it to being tormented 24/7 by a major, invisible giant-sized bully, and wanted to do all she could to prevent the illness sabotaging or maiming her daughter's life in the same way.

Rachel's mum discussed her fears with her husband. They agreed to accept that their family mealtimes would not have a rigid structure. Instead, they opted for a routine pre-meal get-together where they had a drink and discussed the events of the day while preparing their meals in the kitchen. The decision where and with whom to eat was left flexible. Rachel's mother went to see the school nurse and explained that she was concerned that Rachel might be developing anorexia nervosa. The school nurse offered to weigh Rachel each week and to ensure that Rachel sat in the dining room to eat her packed lunch. Rachel and the nurse agreed that the nurse would let her mother know of any weight reduction. Rachel tried hard not to lose weight because she knew her mother would immediately step up efforts to confront any symptoms of anorexia.

In this case, the mother's awareness and early intervention enabled the daughter to override and quash the anorexia thoughts before they became dominant and entrenched.

If you have, or have had, anorexia nervosa and you are aware that your child is developing symptoms, be sure to share these concerns with someone else straightaway. Be open and candid, and acknowledge that you may be over-reacting or being over-sensitive due to your own difficulties and experience, and that you need impartial help. The fact that there is an increased genetic risk does not mean you can do nothing to prevent the illness developing. The environment accounts for something like 50 per cent of the risk. In addition, the genetic vulnerability may need some sort of environmental, psychological or social stress before it expresses itself. By being aware and knowing how to respond, you can help ensure that the family environment is as supportive as possible and that you and your family modify some of the more harmful cultural influences outside the home.

10 Recovery *is* possible

'Will I ever get over it?' 'Yes!' Recovery from anorexia nervosa is indeed possible. Talk about it at every opportunity, maintain hope and a positive attitude – and be patient. Many people unrealistically expect the illness to disappear within a few months. You need to think in terms of years instead of months. Clinically, it is often said the outcome cannot be predicted until five years have passed.

After five years, about half the population with anorexia nervosa will have recovered; 30 per cent will remain quite severely affected by their illness; and 20 per cent will remain underweight and, in the case of girls, without their periods.

What about people in the recovered group? Have they completely got over all their symptoms?

To totally shake off all abnormal attitudes to food and eating is unusual. This is not surprising as anorexic attitudes to food and eating merge into Western cultural attitudes about health, body image and attractiveness. Twenty years after recovering from anorexia, a person may be a normal weight, but remain quite preoccupied with weight and shape. They may say things like: 'If not for my husband and children caring about me, I know I would start losing weight again.'

Even after a two to three-year period of recovery, relapse can and does occur. Vigilance for early warning signs is necessary at all times. Relapse particularly occurs after stressful events, such as losing a job, a relationship breakdown, or death. It can occur as a way of coping with a change in circumstances, such as the empty nest syndrome when children leave home. It can occur if weight loss has been triggered by any reason. For example, after childbirth, the increased stress of looking after a new child, combined with the weight changes after birth, can lead to a relapse. Or perhaps weight loss has occurred following an operation, and the illness behaviours sneak back when you find you have dropped a clothing size and people comment that you look better minus 'those few kilos'.

By being aware of the danger signs and intervening swiftly, you can prevent the illness getting a severe grip. Think of anorexia nervosa as a bully that likes to get you when you are down – it will tempt you at vulnerable times of stress. Be aware, seek help immediately if you recognise the return of anorexia thoughts (e.g., 'I didn't feel like eating breakfast yesterday, and got through the day OK, so I won't eat it today either. Maybe I can skip lunch, too.').

Other people continue to have rigid eating habits and never eat as much or as freely as others.

What happens to those people who don't recover within five years?

People who have struggled with anorexia for more than five years can still shake it off. The illness by now is more firmly entrenched and its behaviours are more difficult, but some people have recovered after more than 30 years of illness. It is never too late. At all times hold on to hope.

A change in the goals for recovery may be necessary for people who have lived with the illness for a long time. As discussed earlier, to expect full recovery after a long illness is not always realistic. However, even partial weight recovery can be of value in that continual hospital admissions are no longer necessary and health and life quality are improved. Conversely, if you continue to suffer from a severe form of anorexia nervosa, the health risk increases.

Specialist treatment centres mainly treat the forms of anorexia nervosa that are severe enough to need hospital treatment. Many other people recover with help from parents, teachers, partners and family doctors. Definitely, early intervention with evidence-based treatment gives best hope of a full recovery.

What factors affect recovery?

These are quite logical and simple.

1. Severity of the anorexia nervosa.

    *   The more weight reduction and the more extreme the emaciation, the worse the outcome.
    *   The longer the illness has gone on before treatment starts, the more it has become entrenched.
    *   When the illness fails to respond to several attempts at treatment, its rigid behaviours become even harder to break down and overcome.

2. Background vulnerability.

    *   Other factors associated with a poorer prognosis are those that indicate problems in adjustment during childhood, before the anorexia began.
    *   Childhood problems such as school refusal and emotional issues.
    *   Difficulty in making friends; experiencing severe shyness or alienation.
    *   Difficulties within the family.

Listing the facts about recovery is not always helpful. Listening to how other people have struggled and overcome their illness can be more useful. Importantly, there is no set pattern. The stories vary considerably.

Miriam

I had been ill for five years and had been in and out of hospital on several occasions. But I failed to gain weight even in hospital. My family was extremely concerned and took me to another clinic. The therapist there suggested that I work on my problems as an outpatient. I was rather surprised at this as, deep down, I felt that I needed inpatient treatment to fight the powerful bully voice in my head. I had absolutely no motivation to start fighting the anorexia nervosa. My weight during the initial four sessions remained extremely low and the therapist remained very anxious about me. Unfortunately I had to give up work after fainting several times.

My GP was so concerned about my physical state that she arranged admission to a local hospital, but the staff were not trained in eating disorder care and had no idea how to confront my illness. I discharged myself within a day. Eventually, after about ten sessions, I began to trust the therapist and was able to open up about underlying problems. My need for perfectionism, for instance, meant that I spent most of the day cleaning the house. I could not see it, but my illness also meant that I had a lot of control over the family and at some level I was aware that I was making their lives miserable in many ways. Mum, for example, couldn't use the kitchen as I regarded it as my territory. I would determine what other people could eat, make the tea and keep the benches and cupboards clean and tidy. A breakthrough in treatment occurred when I was able to see these underlying patterns of behaviour from an outside perspective. I also realised that it was up to me to start working on dismantling and overcoming my problems. I was fed up with being bossed about day and night. No magic solution would be found by entering hospital, or from therapy alone. I had to dig deep, summon the will, and tackle recovery from within. I had a supportive team around me, but to recover I had to do the hard work myself.

Amazingly, I awoke one morning feeling ready to tackle my illness. Enlisting Mum's help, I gradually increased my food intake, and allowed my weight to rise slowly. Amazing things began to happen in response to this weight gain. For instance, my quirky sense of humour returned. My family has always enjoyed playing jokes on each other, seeing the funny side of life and laughing a lot. Due to my illness, I had not laughed for years but now I moved from a passive observer of our family fun to being to a major player. I began to bicycle, got a job and resumed former friendships.

Nicola

I had anorexia nervosa for 15 years. I had been in and out of hospital on ten or more occasions. Often, I was treated under the Mental Health Act. At one stage a tube had to be inserted directly into my stomach for re-feeding.

After this very severe episode, my brother became more involved with me. He was determined to learn more about my illness and help me to recover. He spent more time talking with me and introducing me to his friends. One of his favourite pastimes was 'working-out' at the gym. He said if I ate my three meals and three snacks each day, he would take me along – so we had this agreement which gave me strength to ignore my anorexia bully. On my first visit to the gym the step aerobics class drew my interest. Participating in this class became a new goal. My GP arranged for me to have psychotherapy in a specialist unit. This enabled me to understand how my patterns of behaviour and expectations had been controlled by the anorexia nervosa. With family and therapy support, I was able to withstand the pull of the anorexia bully and maintain a normal eating pattern. I became extremely involved in the step aerobics, progressing to be a tutor and trainer. After five years of unemployment I was able to resume my earlier job of teaching. Overall, I really want to emphasise how my brother's warmth and concern enabled me to start believing that I could recover from the illness. His love helped me to believe in the real me.

Mary

I had struggled with anorexia for 20 years. My husband, like me, was a general practitioner. Many specialists, gastroenterologists and endocrinologists were consulted about my symptoms. Together with my husband, I remained convinced that some medical illness was making me lose weight. Eventually, my GP referred me to a specialist unit. I attended regularly and worked hard at trying to overcome the mystery illness. However, I felt very stuck and was unable to change. My doctor discussed the latest evidence that suggested that olanzepine might have some benefit for people with anorexia nervosa particularly with the driven, compulsive behaviours I had. I slept normally, took the children to school and then returned to bed and slept for several more hours in the morning. Soon I was able to sit down without feeling guilty, and felt more relaxed within the home. In the past I had never been able to sit and watch the television with my children, because the anorexia bully was always driving me to do ironing, cleaning or some other activity. For the first time I was able to fully enjoy simply 'being' with my children and was able to let them have more freedom.

While making good headway on some fronts, I remained extremely concerned about my weight, and even when attending the clinic for the regular weigh-in, I never wanted to know the amount. I remained frightened of seeing evidence that my weight was increasing. Gradually I was able to eat a little more, but the content of my diet remained far from normal. I ate the same foods, in the same quantity, and at the same time, almost every day.

Despite the ongoing issues with weight and food, I improved sufficiently to become much stronger physically. Looking after the children became easier; I was able to be less strict and controlling and enjoy them more. A welcome change was to sit and cuddle, and laugh with them. I was also able to treat myself better, and found pampering sessions an effective diversion against the anorexia bully. Increasingly, I defused the trigger thoughts before they went off, by focusing on an 'in the moment' activity to strengthen the real me – sometimes this meant arranging to catch up with a girlfriend for a coffee, or buying new clothes; other times it meant asserting my newfound self-respect, attending to my feelings and setting limits on other people's demands.

The evidence base for olanzepine is small at the moment. The guidelines developed in many countries such as NICE evaluate the risks and benefits of medication.

Pauline

I arrived at a specialist unit after a crisis referral from my local psychiatric services. My employer insisted that I seek help when I could no longer climb the stairs at work. By the time I was assessed, a severe weakness had developed in my thigh muscles. I had also lost the function of a nerve to one foot and was dragging this foot when walking. Really, I was slightly surprised at all the fuss as I had not noticed anything wrong.

Several years earlier, at university, there was a period when I lost weight. I had counselling, regained the weight and fully recovered. Then I was made redundant after only a short time in my first job, and was let down in a love affair. I managed to obtain another job but by this time had become very concerned and anxious about eating with others at lunchtime. I felt that I had nothing to contribute to the conversation, and began making excuses to skip lunch. In the evening I spent a lot of time preparing my food, which was mainly vegetables and fruit.

I didn't realise I was ill and was shocked when the specialist psychiatrist described the severity of my condition and the medical dangers that I was facing.

Inpatient treatment was strongly recommended but I really did not want this. Fortunately the doctor agreed that I could stay at home if someone would be there to look after me and supervise the meals. Dad came to the rescue. He travelled several hundred miles within two days to attend a meeting with the doctor and me. Dad hadn't seen me for a while and was shocked at my thinness. He helped me realise that I was sick. We made a plan whereby I had to eat every few hours. Under his unwavering watch and further encouraged by the treatment sessions, I managed to stick to our plan and gradually gained weight. Dad's love and the care of the therapist enabled me to recognise that my health was in a dangerous condition and became determined to work on recovery.

Karen

I am 27 years old. I am the only daughter of two academics and have an older brother who is considered very bright. Mum is of Central European origin, and although I have grown up in the United Kingdom, my family has remained quite socially isolated, focusing instead on pursuing high academic standards. I felt I could not talk to Mum, who doted on my brother, but I was 'Daddy's little girl'. Anorexia nervosa developed during my A-level year. I was trying to gain control over my life, as I felt my parents were ruling it for me. On leaving school I was offered a place in college but had difficulty making friends and felt that I did not fit in.

Unhappy, I dropped out and obtained a job in the Civil Service where I have remained since. My anorexia nervosa waxed and waned over this ten-year period and I received many different forms of treatment, ranging from hypnotherapy to psychoanalytic psychotherapy. A year ago, I was finally admitted to hospital for the first time, at age 26. I attribute my recovery to this period of inpatient treatment, as I felt unable to withstand the bossy thoughts of the anorexia bully on my own. Treatment included family therapy and this enabled Mum and I to start communicating on an adult level. Feeling accepted by Mum has meant a lot to me. We go shopping together and meet occasionally for lunch. I remain in good health a year after discharge from the eating disorder unit. One minor relapse occurred during a period of depression, which was arrested as soon as I realised the illness thoughts were having too much say. I love my family and feeling close to them gives me strength to be me!

Jackie

I am a 25-year-old student nurse and had never been concerned with my weight or shape until the breakup of a relationship in which I felt betrayed. I initially lost my appetite and this led to weight loss. During this period I confided in friends, but began to feel I was boring them. They noticed that I had lost a lot of weight, said I looked ill, and were concerned. But I thought they were carrying on over nothing and withdrew further into myself. My weight plummeted and I was referred for outpatient psychotherapy. It was during this period that a special 'light bulb' moment occurred. I was walking through a beautiful grassy park on a sunny summer's day when I suddenly realised that the only reason I was miserable was because I was not allowing myself to eat. From that moment on, recovery began. I gradually regained weight, my periods returned and I have been well since. I enjoy a busy social life. My maintenance 'medicine' is three meals and three snacks a day. It makes all the difference!

Section Three

For families, carers and friends

11 Helping to eliminate the eating disorder

Family members and friends can together provide a network of love, care and understanding to help the sufferer escape the eating disorder trap. They can acquire knowledge and coping skills to challenge and encourage the dismantling, rather than strengthening, of the eating disorder symptoms.

This chapter aims to introduce some of the new understanding about how an eating disorder can draw the family into a pattern of behaviours that keeps the eating disorder firmly embedded in its victim. Anorexia nervosa has a profound impact on other people, both through the direct effect of the symptoms and indirectly by changing the person you know and love. Your loved one may appear to have been taken over by an 'eating disorder bully' who sits resolutely in their brain, feeding them misinformation. Learning to recognise when behaviours are driven by the eating disorder, rather than the person's true self, is helpful. This skill is called externalising. Importantly, your reactions to this bully can change the course the illness takes. We provide an outline of what has been found to be helpful or harmful and how you can best provide support and guidance through the many eating disorder traps.

Remember

- *Parents are not to blame* – repeat this, 'I am not to blame', until you accept and believe it. You have not done anything to cause the problem. Hit the delete button on 'blame' and 'guilt' at all times. Guilt is harmful both for you and for your child, for it will 'feed' the eating disorder symptoms.
- *Anorexia nervosa is not a choice* – you cannot choose to develop this illness. Although food restriction may start as a deliberate act, the secondary problems – especially those in the brain – make recovery difficult.

Truths

- Parents, partners and close others can be an important part of the solution. Developing skills to manage the illness is possible and can have broader benefits. We are constantly impressed with how quickly and effectively carers pick up the psychological principles that professionals take six or more years to master.
- People with eating disorders say that one of the few things that can give them pleasure and reward is time with family. Keep this in mind.
- Social isolation easily develops and is toxic for the person with the illness. Time with family can break this loneliness.
- Do not try to be a perfect carer. Scheduling time out to relax and recharge is essential. Having support readily available is essential.
- Often family members have the same strengths in analysis and persistence as the person with an eating disorder. These traits can be used to help recovery.

• We cannot emphasise enough the importance of a consistent joint approach. The more heads that are used in this recovery process the better. Teamwork and collaboration by everyone involved is crucial to outsmart and overcome the eating disorder.

Breaking processes that maintain the illness

We will describe how skills-based caring can interrupt vicious circles that 'trap' people with an eating disorder and those close to them.

When someone we love is ill, we naturally want to care for them and somewhat spoil them. For short-term viral illnesses, this response assists recovery. However, for emotional problems, the reverse can be true. We pose some questions about processes that commonly occur and suggest why they can be harmful.

Question: **Does the person with an Eating Disorder (Ed) bully you about what, when and how you eat? Are you bullied about when and how you can use the kitchen and/or bathroom? Perhaps the Ed controls what, when and how you shop? And about when and how mealtimes are arranged? Does the Ed stipulate the portions or ingredients?**

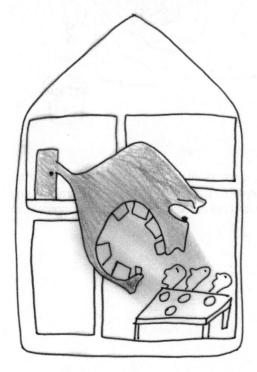

The Ed bully

The downside of walking on eggshells and submitting to the control of the 'anorexic bully' is that anorexia nervosa bullying is rewarded. The anorexic bully finds it gratifying to have its commands obeyed and carries on. Moreover, the person dominated by the illness does not learn how to think and respect the thoughts and feelings of others. A trap is sprung.

Question: **There again, perhaps you are trying to hide negative consequences of Ed behaviour by clearing up mess, dealing with bathroom problems, buying more food, and cooking a meal that you know is nutritionally inadequate? Perhaps you are into self-denial about evidence of antisocial behaviour such as hoarding, stealing or addictions?**

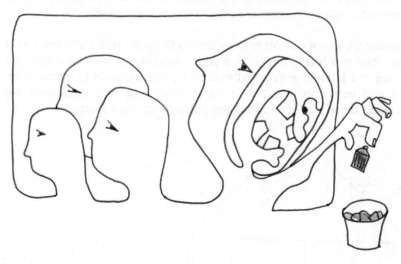

Ignoring

Ignoring, covering up, avoiding unpleasant aspects of the eating disorder prevents Ed experiencing negative consequences. When unrestrained and unchallenged, the hold of the illness is re-enforced and derails any momentum for change.

Question: **Have you been drawn into giving reassurance or been sucked into obsessional rituals or compulsive concerns?**

Giving reassurance

The problem with giving reassurance on tap is that it allows avoidance of anxiety but at a cost of dependence. You become your child's shield against the world but a backlash will be that part of them will resent being so trapped.

Encourage the development of more mature ways of emotional regulation by a careful analysis of what the feeling is signalling and how the need can be met.

Your reaction to the illness

Eating disorder symptoms and their consequences – for example, changes in personality and deterioration in physical health – may lead you to respond sometimes with critical confrontations. Unfortunately, this may cause the person with the eating disorder to feel increasingly misunderstood, alienated and stigmatised, and may result in them being drawn further into eating disorder behaviour.

Animal metaphors (jelly fish, ostrich, kangaroo, rhinoceros and terrier) help to explain how these instinctive reactions can be unhelpful. A veritable menagerie emerges as we metamorphose from one animal state to another in a desperate attempt to remedy the situation. Each animal analogy may be your default way of coping with stress, or part of your natural temperament; for example, over-protective, logical, and overtly emotional or avoidant. In order to change these responses, you may have to challenge yourself and experiment with trying out new responses that do not feel natural or spontaneous. Don't worry if you do not succeed at first. Try to remember to keep looking to the bigger picture. Everything is practice.

Jellyfish: too much emotion and too little control

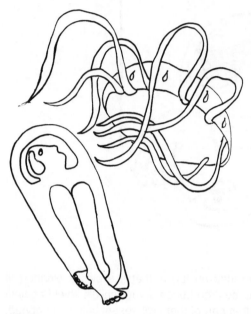

Jellyfish

Some carers may be unable to regulate their own intense emotional responses to the anorexia. Their distress and anger is transparent to all. In this sea of emotion it is hard to steer a clear path. Also, like a jellyfish, overt anger and anxiety can exert a poisonous sting with the same emotions being mirrored in your child. Unfortunately, this helps to increase the anorexic hold. The downside is that these 'sad and mad' emotions escalate, causing tears, tempers, sleepless nights and exhaustion in both you and your child.

Often this high level of emotion can lead to worry. Worry itself can be productive or non-productive. If you are worrying a lot, ask yourself why and work out whether it is productive or unproductive worry.

Worry can be productive if you have a concern or problem that you can do something about right now or in the very near future. This type of worry usually takes the form of a question that has an answer. Therefore you can apply strategies such as problem solving, coping statements or support from others to take decisive action and manage the anxiety-provoking situation.

However, worry is unproductive when it involves 'what if?' questions over which you have little or no control, or questions that cannot be answered yet. If your worry is of this unproductive kind, use strategies to manage it rather than squander your limited brain resource on a fruitless task. For example, a more helpful approach involves making sure that this unproductive effort is time limited – allow a set amount of worry time (e.g., between 2pm and 3pm in the afternoon, perhaps in combination with a walk). Use more productive ways to manage stress such as mindfulness, breathing techniques, distraction or exercise.

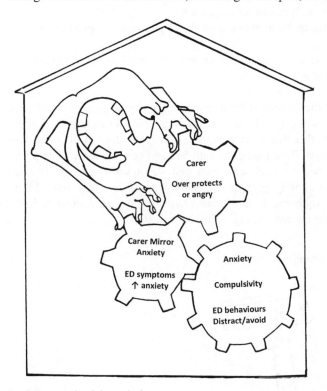

Anxiety cascade vicious circle

Regulating your emotional reaction can be difficult if you hold some false interpretations about the anorexia, high levels of self-blame, or perfectionist expectations about your role as a parent. Emotion regulation is also difficult when you are tired, tense and stressed. Consider the following points in two ways – as yourself and as if you are a kind compassionate friend looking in at yourself:

- Reflect on your jellyfish tendencies. How do they make you feel?
- What are the effects of these responses on you? On others?
- How important is it that you work on your 'jellyfish' responses?
- If you were advising a friend with the same problem, what would you suggest? How would you help them take the step to modify and change their jellyfish behaviour?
- What beliefs do you need to work on in order for this change to happen?
- How can protect yourself from getting total emotional burn out?

- Brainstorm scheduling some fun into your life and ways to nurture yourself. Take up a hobby, catch up with friends or take a walk while listening to music. Try writing your ideas down and then timetable this relax-and-recharge 'me' time into each day. This approach will encourage your child to find healthy ways of coping when you are away. You are modelling how to build a positive resource to help with emotional regulation.
- The fact that you are reading this book shows that you are open to new ideas. Well done!
- Talking to others and seeking advice are wise ways to help regulate your emotional response.

Important! Each of the aforementioned 'important' points applies to you! If your emotional reaction is taking over, this will be mirrored and exaggerated by the illness responses. Rather like in an aircraft emergency, you need to put on your own oxygen mask first. Role modelling self-care and compassion will help your child think about their own self-care as a first step towards change. Be their inspiration: work on coming up with ideas on how to achieve 'me' time. Taking care of your own wellbeing in both your physical and your mental health is important. Well done for considering taking the first step.

Ostrich: avoiding emotion

Ostrich

The ostrich finds it hard to cope with the volcanic situation that often arises when confronting anorexia nervosa. Emotions and the complexities of human behaviour are too chaotic and confusing. The ostrich literally prefers to bury their head in the sand. This is something they know they confidently can do, enabling them to avoid facing situations that seem too hard. The downside is that the person with the eating disorder may misinterpret this approach, seeing you as uncaring and end up feeling unloved. Self-esteem ebbs away. Additionally, the concealment of emotions sets an unhelpful example to follow. Setting an example of emotional honesty and illustrating that having emotions is normal and acceptable human behaviour will help your child come to terms with their own difficulties with emotional expression. Living with others who can and are able to convey their feelings with words will help the person with the eating disorder change their only way of articulating their emotions: through food. Often we know we are aroused but we do not know what the exact emotion is and what need it is signalling. People with eating disorders often need help with recognising their feelings and you may be able to provide this help.

Ask yourself the following questions and also answer these questions as if you are a kind, compassionate friend looking on:

- Reflect on your ostrich tendencies. Have they succeeded in helping you and those you love feel safe and secure?
- Can you take steps to become less of an ostrich?
- Who can support you in experimenting with new responses and help you reflect on your progress in adapting to this non-ostrich role?
- What would you want this person to do or say? A list of suggestions is often useful.
- What do you think about involving others in helping you make the necessary changes?
- How do you feel about making these changes? Are you ready to hold your head high and share your feelings?

Important! Change can be difficult and uncomfortable. Engaging the help of a supportive family member/friend to support you in your quest may be worthwhile. Think about your own self-esteem and how role-modelling confidence in facing rather than avoiding difficulties might help your child experiment with changing their own behaviour. The fact you are reading this sheet and considering these questions is already a huge step.

Kangaroo: trying to make everything right

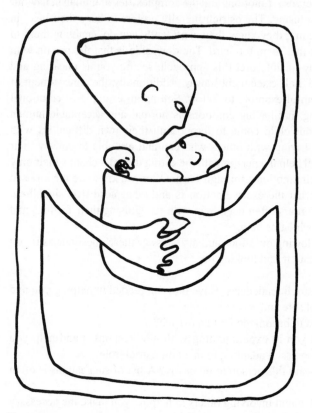

Kangaroo

The kangaroo does everything to protect by taking over all aspects of the sufferer's life. They treat the person with the eating disorder with kid gloves, letting them jump into the kangaroo pouch in an effort to avoid any upset or stress. The downside of this type of caring is that it denies the sufferer the chance to learn how to approach and master life's challenges. They feel safe only when living in this limbo land, suspended in a child-like role, and are unable to visualise, let alone take steps to fully engage in the world or taking up the mantle of adulthood.

Ask yourself the following questions and also answer them as if you are a kind, compassionate friend looking on:

• Reflect on your kangaroo responses. How are they working for you?
• What difficulties are you encountering? Give an example of what is not working for you.
• What aspects of your kangaroo behaviour can you experiment with? For instance, are you afraid to say: 'No'?

- How important is it for you to address some of your kangaroo responses?
- Think back to one of your kangaroo behaviours in recent weeks. How can you change that behaviour a little? What would be the first step when this situation arises again? What will you say? Role play or writing a script can help prepare you.
- Who can help you judge whether you are being over protective?

Important! Change is tough. Remember to congratulate yourself after attempting each change! Taking safe risks is a key aspect of change. Taking baby steps to achieve change is fine. Keep at it. If you are not taking flak, you are not over the target. Your role modelling of respect and confidence will connect with your child's innate wisdom and help them rebuild their self-esteem.

Rhinoceros: using force to win the day

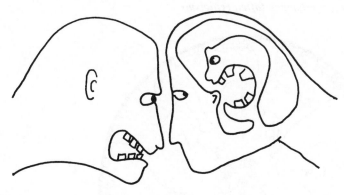

Rhinoceros

Fuelled by stress, exhaustion and frustration, or simply one's own temperament, the rhino attempts to persuade and convince by argument and confrontation. The downside is that even when your child does obey, confidence to do so independently is not developed. In fact, the more likely response to a rhino 'in a china shop' is to argue back with a strong anorexic voice. Unfortunately, the more the anorexic bully retaliates, the more the anorexia nervosa identity consolidates, strengthens and dominates the mind of the sufferer.

Ask yourself the following questions and also answer these questions as if you are a kind, compassionate friend looking on:

- Reflect on your rhinoceros responses. Are they working for you?
- What difficulties are you encountering?
- How can you avoid these obstacles?
- What might be the repercussions of changing your rhino response, both positive and negative?

- While contracts can work in a 'crisis situation', and providing rewards for positive behaviour may be helpful, have you considered motivating and encouraging your child to develop independent thinking by letting them make decisions and come up with their own innovative solutions?
- What can you do for yourself to lower your anxiety, stress or anger levels?
- Set a goal for yourself with regards to this. How do you think this will make you feel?

Important! Remember that the more you argue for change, the more you give the eating disorder opportunity to argue for no change. This allows anorexia nervosa to embed itself more deeply. Keep calm and carry on. A key skill is to allow your child opportunity to present their own arguments as to why change is needed. However, there are non-negotiable boundaries – for instance, prolonged starvation is toxic and needs to be arrested.

Terrier: using persistence (often criticism)

Terrier

The terrier persistently criticises, cajoles, nags and tries to wear out the anorexic bully. The downside of this terrier type behaviour is that the person with the eating disorder either tunes out to what they perceive as irritating white noise or their morale is sapped to the point where they lose the inner resource to face the rich tapestry of life without an anorexic identity.

Ask yourself the following questions and also answer these questions as if you are a kind compassionate friend looking on:

- Reflect on your terrier tendencies. How do they make you and the family feel? Are they working and helping your child feel safe enough to leave anorexia?
- What are the effects of this terrier response on you? And on others?
- How important do you consider the need to work on your 'terrier' type behaviour?
- If advising a friend with the same problem, what would you say to them?
- What steps can you take to develop rewarding communication? Remember, a key skill is trying to listen to what your child might be struggling to say.
- What beliefs do you need to work on in order to facilitate this productive communication?
- How can you take steps to be an active listener? Chapter 8 of *Skills-based Learning for Caring for a Loved One with an Eating Disorder* (Treasure et al., 2007) describes how to improve communication. It involves OARS: Open questions, Affirmations, Reflections and Summaries. This technique is worth trying!
- The fact that you are reading this book shows that you are open to new ideas. Well done! What specifically can you do now to get started with these different patterns of responding?

Important! The anorexia nervosa itself is rather like a terrier constantly criticising the sufferer, telling them they are not good enough, and that they need to try harder to do what it wants. Role modelling calm compassion and firm non-negotiable limits will help your child feel confident enough to take a stance with their anorexic voice. Be aware that suppression of worries can be difficult and nagging may slip through – try reducing this risk by splitting your attention with another task such as driving. This can help you listen.

Poisonous polarised positions

A problem that can arise is that family members react to each other's animal response by trying to compensate. For example, a father may respond to his wife's kangaroo reaction by becoming more distant and ostrich-like. Or a father may respond to his wife's jellyfish response by becoming a rhino. Or vice versa.

The answer is to work together to find the middle ground – the goldilocks solution – and for your behaviour to become more like that of the inspirational animals.

Inspirational animals

Of all the animals in the animal kingdom, we want you to aspire to be a St Bernard for warmth and compassion in the face of danger and a dolphin for its wisdom and hands-off style of support.

Dolphin: just enough caring and control

Dolphin

An optimal way of helping someone with an eating disorder is to gently nudge them along. Imagine your child is at sea. The anorexic identity is their life vest. They are unwilling and too afraid to give up the safety of this life vest while living in the turbulent waters of anorexia. You are the dolphin, nudging them to safety, at times swimming ahead, leading the way, showing them new vistas, at other times swimming alongside with encouragement, or even quietly swimming behind.

If you want to go fast, walk alone; if you want to go far, walk together.

African proverb

St Bernard: just enough compassion and consistency

St Bernard

Another optimal caring response is one of calmness, warmth and compassion. This involves accepting and processing the pain resulting from what is lost through anorexia and developing reserves of kindness, gentleness and love. St Bernard instils hope in the child that they can change, that there is a future full of possibility beyond the eating disorder. St Bernard responds consistently. He is unfailing, reliable and dependable in all circumstances. He has good antennae attuned to the welfare and safety of those who are lost – calm, warm and nurturing.

> Perseverance, secret of all triumphs.
>
> Victor Hugo

Turning up the warmth

People with an eating disorder are supersensitive to threat and criticism and fail to respond to warmth, kindness and compassion. They may even feel guilty if they try to do this. A positive emotional resource is needed to conquer fears and regulate emotions wisely. Time with caring family members or friends in a warm and positive atmosphere is essential. Making time to focus on all things positive is as important as trying to tackle the eating disorder head on. An important task is to increase your presence as someone who can be trusted, and relied on, in your child's life.

All families have rich resources to do this by noticing the beauty, goodness, humour and other virtues in everyday life: sharing conversations, sharing enjoyable activities, having fun together and reliving happy memories. Noticing acts of kindness and expressing gratitude can help to remedy the negative bias in attention. Remember, your unrelenting love and devoted relationship is bigger and stronger than the eating disorder and can be a force for change.

Care for the carers

However, eating disorders are exhausting and you need care and support in order to nurture. Assistance from others is essential. Friends, family or a support group can provide this help. You may face a few obstacles like these:

- *Not wanting to be a burden or to be blamed.* Other people like to be helpful and may even feel honoured to be asked. Asking for assistance helps you sidestep blame and shame.
- *Not wanting to be disloyal to your child.* The primary and paramount need is to be an effective, secure carer. Avoidance is the default position of an eating disorder. Calm, considered action – such as when and how to ask for help – is an important life lesson.
- *Fear of anger or contempt from your child.* The anorexic bully will use this weapon. Stand up to it. Go ahead and ask for help. You need support to give strength and balance.

In the next section we give tips to help you promote change but remember, always, that love and warmth go a long way. You need to decide how active you want to be and how much you will let others help, too.

How to be an effective mentor to support change

The following ideas are derived from established psychological principles about ways of helping people change. The process involves gentle guidance and compassionate coaching with a fixed focus on the essence of recovery. Remember, not eating is non-negotiable.

Helping someone to change is not easy. Nagging (terrier) or imposing change aggressively (rhino), or doing it for them (kangaroo) can hinder change if the person has mixed feelings. The eating disorder has a very loud and persistent 'voice'. If it senses a weakness or doubt, it may push your child in the opposite direction.

A clear focus, cut through detail

You may want to change an array of behaviours. Focus on one or two at a time (in eating disorders these are often eating and vomiting). To make the process explicit sit down with your supporter and write down all unhealthy behaviours on slips of paper. Next sort the slips into baskets. The largest pile will be for those you will ignore, at least for now. The middle-sized pile will be for those you are willing to be flexible and negotiate over. The smallest pile will be for behaviour you will no longer tolerate and requires your attention right now.

Concise communication

Your message must be sufficiently clear to be heard through the fog of starvation and the sirens of the eating disorder voice. A good idea can be to write down your short message so that you stick to the script and it can be retained. Keep calm and restrict it to what you will do. For example:

> The eating disorder is an unbearable intruder in our family life. We will do all we can to change the situation. We will not hide what is going on and we will get help. We will resist the following behaviours:
>
> 1. Not eating
> 2. Vomiting
>
> We are doing this because we love you and we want the best for you.

Change the routine

Susan's parents decided to turn the world, that the eating disorder had been thriving in, on its head. So the father took charge of cooking meals and feeding Susan. Her mother and siblings went to visit various family members over the weekends. Dad and Susan stayed behind. Dad explained that he loved her and he was going to rescue her and care for her by providing a different environment so that the anorexia became unsettled. He cooked together with Susan and on occasions they went out for a meal. His expectations were that Susan would eat and join in activities he planned after meals such as a walk in the park or around the block. They would have conversations about interesting, curious or pleasant events that they had experienced themselves or were in the daily news.

Allow your child opportunity to create strategies

Set aside a regular time for conversations where you gently encourage your child to talk about what they can do to help facilitate a change in their behaviour. At the same time remain firm that you will not put up with eating disorder behaviour: 'We are not prepared to allow the eating disorder behaviours to damage you. We are here to solve the problem. We will sit and wait until you suggest a solution.' Remain quiet and wait for suggestions. Listen to the suggestions and plan an experiment to give them a chance. Do not allow yourself to get drawn into anorexic talk.

The following questions can be put to your child on other occasions:

- What can you visualise yourself doing in the future?
- What advice would you give a friend or a daughter in a similar situation to you right now?
- Have you read about strategies that have worked for other people? Let's draw two ruler scales. We will label one scale 'readiness or confidence to change' and the second scale 'ability to see a change through'. What score do you give yourself out of ten on each of these scales? What will help you achieve a higher score? How can I help? Can you imagine making a small change today?

Revisiting and revising these motivation scales can be a helpful way of reviewing progress and maintaining the momentum towards recovery.

The person with the eating disorder may be more comfortable and able to talk about change in certain settings or situations. For example, if the family home is currently a place of conflict, somewhere neutral (such as sitting on a park bench or driving) may evoke more confidence or readiness to consider talk about change.

Be alert for any glimmers of change, or talk about change. Paying special attention to these 'windows of opportunity' increases the odds that more change will happen. Continually motivate and encourage your loved one. Recovering from an eating disorder is a journey, not a destination.

Recovery is not just about food. Change involves becoming more flexible and able to see the bigger picture. It involves becoming more mindful about emotional factors. It also means being able to see things from many perspectives and to connect with other people. So keep a look out for steps and opportunities leading towards these behaviours.

Prompting for a behavioural resolution and planning it out in great detail as if designing a storyboard, visualising each detail with very small steps, is often a good start.

Write a letter or put a few lines on a flash card to tell your child about their positive attributes, things that make you love them, make them special and make you smile, things you miss about them now that they are unwell. This may help them gain a sliver of vital insight, perspective and motivation at a time when their illness has narrowed their focus to food.

Encourage your child to write down plans and goals. This big picture activity helps them to step outside the confusion of mixed feelings. Additionally, noting their aspirations and future ambitions will help them through times when their illness dominates and their world shrinks again to eating, food, weight and calories.

Sometimes looking to the future is impossible and inconceivable. At such times, looking to the past to find a place of contentment might help. A holiday photo or a picture of a place where your child has felt comfortable, safe and at ease may inspire them to try recreating and reclaiming those feelings.

Emotions and feelings can be difficult for a person with an eating disorder to express or regulate. Pinpointing exactly how they feel at a particular moment can be a challenge when emotions are frozen by the illness. Empathy and emotional wisdom are needed. Remember, regulating emotions is hard for those in 'flight or fight mode' secondary to an eating disorder. Remaining calm, perhaps with cool-off time, may be needed.

Using prompts as a reminder to perform a behaviour, may help. For example, sending a text message when it is time for a snack.

Rewards and goal setting

Another psychological technique that can be helpful if there is a good, warm, trusting relationship is to plan a contract about goals to aim for, with rewards for progress in meeting the goals. The style should be compassionate and collaborative with the emphasis on action and behaviour that has occurred rather than talk, which often leads to a circular dance going nowhere.

Conclusion

In this chapter we have described how each member of the family can become trapped and isolated by an eating disorder, leading to loneliness and despair.

Key problems:

- The symptoms of an eating disorder (starvation, vomiting) compromise the organ needed to recover (the brain).
- The longer the symptoms persist the more the symptoms become embedded.

- Symptom change: stopping starvation and vomiting is the first priority.
- This is not a six-week or even six-month fix.
- Expect the eating disorder to project extreme resistance. Especially initially.

Key solutions:

- Collaborative brainpower – the more people who work together on the problem the better.
- Compassionate care can help the person with anorexia nervosa to climb up the slippery slope to recovery.
- A big picture perspective with a focus on the values of life rather than worrying about small details is essential.
- Flexibility can help broaden and build a new identity and confident personality in the post-eating disorder world.
- Cherish and relish green shoots of hope and growth.

12 Pulling together as a family

Families pass through various stages during the diagnosis, treatment and recovery phases experienced with anorexia nervosa and it is impossible to write a chapter to address every scenario. Nevertheless, certain ground rules apply to almost every case. You will need to use your judgement to decide what is appropriate for your family.

Being the parent of someone with anorexia nervosa is difficult. The illness disrupts family life. Amid this turmoil, it is crucial that you continue to have your own life and don't neglect your partner or other children. Make sure you set aside regular time to spend with them and to pursue your own interests. You may find meeting the parents of other sufferers helpful. The support of your friends and relatives also can be invaluable.

Remember that you are a parent rather than a best friend to your child who has developed anorexia nervosa. Sufferers from anorexia nervosa are often caring, sensitive people and it can be tempting to unburden yourself to them. You may look to your child for support as another woman if the men in your life are not being supportive or are causing problems. Unfortunately, conflict can follow the resulting divided loyalties and abuse of trust. If your child has become your main confidante, try to build on links with women friends. Don't be surprised or hurt if your child does not want to discuss all the details of their life or treatment with you; it is normal and healthy for adolescents to have secrets from their parents and this is part of the process of normal separation.

Many marriages are under strain in our Western society. Old values and expectations have been questioned and overturned. Over one-third of marriages end in divorce. Many people, however, struggle with difficulties within their marriage to find a solution. Although we do not think that difficulties within marriage cause eating disorders, they make coping with an eating disorder much more difficult.

Consistency is essential. As a parent, it is important to provide your children with a framework of rules for living. They may object and fight against the rules but this is appropriate. Adolescents need rules to rebel against. Your child will feel more secure if you are able to take a firm stand on what you believe. Try to make sure that you know what you believe and the reasons underlying this belief so that when it comes to negotiation you know how far you are prepared to bend. If you have a partner, make sure the two of you present a united front to your child with anorexia. Avoid being drawn into making decisions when you know your partner will disapprove. Remember that a united front is vital in confronting and breaking down the manipulative behaviours of the eating disorder.

Have regular meetings outside mealtimes to decide the rules. Many families of adolescents, particularly those in which everyone is very busy, find it useful to set aside at least half an hour a week where they all sit together to discuss family issues. These meetings will vary: they may be used to set ground rules, ask for help, review the week's events or plan the week's meals. Developing a checklist of rules for family life is often helpful. Although no two families are the same and there are many different ways of living together successfully, certain rules are helpful to adopt when a family member is suffering from anorexia nervosa. Without firm boundaries, the illness can run riot.

Basic rules

1. Accept that family members respect each other. Therefore, the parents respect the child's move towards independence. The children respect the need of their parents to spend part of their lives separately from the children. Each parent respects each other's need to lead part of their life independently.
2. Each family decides what behaviour is unacceptable and set limits on it. Specifically, parents as adults place limits on their children's behaviour.
3. Parents cooperate and enhance, rather than hinder, each other's efforts.
4. Parents share the responsibility for their child equally (even if one takes the lead, the other provides support in other ways to maintain the balance of care).
5. As much as is possible with a debilitating illness such as anorexia nervosa, parents ensure that their child is moving towards independence.
6. Parents ensure they have regular time away from caring to enjoy each other's company.

The following case examples illustrate what can happen when these basic rules are forgotten. Perhaps they remind you of what happens in your home:

Jennifer

Jennifer, aged 17, had suffered from anorexia nervosa for four years. She had been in hospital five times. Jennifer was proud but also rather afraid of her father who was a successful businessman. She was concerned that she would not meet his standards. He was distressed and puzzled by Jennifer's 'eating' problem. Her illness was one area of his life he couldn't control. He was often away on business leaving his wife with their daughter's day-to-day management. Jennifer's mother became exhausted and was often weeping when he telephoned home each evening. When at home he tried to help Jennifer eat but he even seemed to make a mess of this. Things got worse when his wife screamed: 'Why don't you do something helpful for a change?' He sat patiently and watched while Jennifer shredded a slice of cucumber into 50 pieces and slid her hard-boiled egg around the plate. After two hours he lost his temper and started to shout at Jennifer. In his anger he slapped her. He had never before hit her. Both Jennifer and her dad were shocked and upset. He left the house to calm down. His wife's response was sarcastic: 'How can you do this to our child who is ill? She is not one of your employees.' After this episode, the dad stopped trying to help. Jennifer's mother oscillated between trying hard to be friendly and sympathetic, and becoming distant and sulky when they felt overwhelmed and hopeless. This impasse lasted for more than a year and Jennifer required two more admissions.

With much patience and tolerance, the family began to work together. Jennifer's father arranged to arrive at work late each Monday morning so he and his wife could have a set time to discuss progress. They agreed on a joint plan that they both could handle. Gradually, Jennifer's mother was able to distance herself emotionally if Jennifer failed to finish their meal. Instead of feeling hurt or upset they noted it on the agenda for the next week. Similarly, when Jennifer's father supervised a meal, he no longer felt it was a point of honour to ensure that he had won. At their Monday meetings the parents exchanged observations about what had seemed helpful and planned to test alternative approaches the following week. The parents began to laugh together at mistakes they felt they had made and warmly responded when one of them felt dispirited. The snipes and sneers of the previous two years vanished. Jennifer responded to this lighter atmosphere by gaining weight.

In other families, parents with long-standing difficulties may face extreme difficulty in working together. Here are some examples.

Vanessa

Vanessa developed anorexia nervosa when she was 13. She lost weight quickly and was admitted to an adolescent unit. The parents indicated that they had difficulty working together. In a private session Vanessa's mother, Hilary, told the therapist about their marital problems. They described a turning point in their marriage when her husband, Bill, hit her during an argument. Outraged by this show of violence and determined not to remain a victim, Hilary made plans to become financially more secure. She took up a teaching job when Vanessa was aged seven. The family moved into a new, big house and both incomes were necessary to pay the mortgage. Hilary was earning more than Bill but still had to negotiate with him over purchases. This led to frequent rows and several times, after he had been drinking, Bill hit her. Talks of separation were taking place when Vanessa's eating disorder began. Shocked, the parents put their marital difficulties on hold and tried to work together to help their child. Their efforts, however, were fraught with problems. Hilary was frightened of delegating to Bill, as she feared that he would hit Vanessa. She said nothing about this fear but tried to shield Vanessa from Bill's anger. With parents so split, Vanessa's anorexia flourished.

Carla

Carla developed anorexia nervosa when she was 15. Her brother, who was seven years older, had left home after finishing university. Carla was very close to their mother, Jenny, who complained a lot about David, her husband. David was always out – he worked long hours and, instead of coming home, preferred to unwind in the evening with his friends at the local pub. Jenny had difficulty communicating with David about this. She would talk and try to engage him in conversation but he would remain silent. With nobody else to talk to, Carla became Jenny's sounding board. Carla, however, was too young to understand the world of adult relationships. Her mother never talked about the good things she got from her marriage and Carla, therefore, built up a very one-sided picture, which fuelled her tendency to think in black-and-white terms. She thought the simple answer to easing the stress would be for her mum to divorce her dad. She found her mother's obvious ambivalence – of criticising their father but doing nothing about it – frustrating. Eventually, Carla took matters into her own hands and started to behave as she thought her mother should. She refused to talk to her dad and 'divorced' him from her life by taking rather drastic measures to establish independence – including leaving home to avoid financial support. As for her mother, Carla considered her to be almost prostituting herself by staying in the marriage. Because Carla refused to talk to her dad or even be in the same room, it was impossible to get the parents to work together to help their child.

In the marriages described in these examples, the (basic) rules have been broken. In each of the families the first rule (i.e. that partners respect each other) is broken. Jennifer's parents had adopted diverse roles but showed a tendency to undervalue each other. In Bill and Hilary's marriage, there was overt sexism. Bill had difficulty adjusting to his wife's new assertiveness and expectations. He expected to be able to exert his dominance over the family by physical and financial means. Jenny did not respect the privacy of her husband David by talking about him to Carla, and behaved inappropriately when she used Carla as a sounding board for their difficulties. David and Jenny needed to try to communicate with each other.

Improving communication

You will find that the need to communicate with each other and your child is emphasised throughout this book. Making time to talk may seem an obvious point, but often rules of social interaction are ignored at home.

Communication is more effective when:

1. Only one person speaks at a time.
2. A person is talked to rather than talked about.
3. Speaking time is divided evenly.
4. Time is taken to understand what each other is saying.
5. Positive feelings are expressed.

Rules 4 and 5 need a little more explanation because they are less obvious and yet cause great difficulties. Misunderstandings and misinterpretations can easily occur. This is because we all have our own assumptions or automatic reactions, which are not necessarily shared with others. Men and women have different communication styles and this can lead to friction. One way to prevent misunderstandings is to check that you have understood the intention of what was said. You can do this by paraphrasing, to check that the meaning is understood, or even repeating what was said. This can signal to the other person that they have been heard. Often in families, each member carries on speaking about his or their own agenda without evidence that they are considering the views of others.

All families have difficulties expressing positive sentiments to each other. We tend to be most grumpy and impolite at home. Positive comments have been revealed to occur one out of ten at home, whereas the frequency of negative comments is nine out of ten. When families are under stress, they make more negative statements. Counteract this by finding positive things to note and make sure your comments are heard clearly.

Here are a few tips to help you improve positive comments at home:

- Look at the person you are speaking to and speak in a warm tone.
- Tell them exactly what they did to please you.
- Let them know how this made you feel.

For example: 'I am pleased that you were able to eat your meal with us tonight. It makes me feel that we are moving forward.'

Similarly, if you want to request a change in behaviour, do so positively. Follow similar steps:

- Tell the person how you would expect to feel if they perform that behaviour.
- Look at the person and speak in a firm but friendly tone.
- Describe exactly what you would like the other person to do.

Examples of openers:

- 'I'd like you to. . .'
- 'I'd be most grateful if you would. . .'
- 'I'd be pleased if you. . .'

Negative expressions

Bottling up negative thoughts is pointless and harmful, and repetitive comments on the negative rarely produce a change in behaviour. The best tack is to delay expressing negative comments, frustrations and disappointments until they can be said calmly and clearly.

Follow the same rules as for positive communication:

- Look at the person you are talking to.
- Describe clearly the behaviour that upset you.
- Let them know how it made you feel.

For example: 'Sally I felt upset and cut off when you ran out of the room last night and then refused to talk. Can we talk now so we can both understand what was going on?'

Play it cool: cut the criticism

Illnesses and difficulties cause us all to get upset. Anorexia nervosa can be one of the most frustrating illnesses. The cure appears to be easy and straightforward: eating. Yet putting it into practice can be so hard! Also, recovery is slow. Getting over anorexia nervosa is not like getting over flu. Parents who are watching anorexia nervosa destroy their child's life can feel terrified and miserable. This mixture of anger, fear, despair and frustration can easily boil over and worsen the situation. Another vicious circle! Is the following scenario familiar?

Susan

Susan was gradually overcoming her eating disorder. She had started to eat meals with the family. One day she was eating quiche and salad with her parents. The quiche was a challenge. Her mother suddenly asked: 'When will you stop having a nervous breakdown over a piece of cheese?'

Susan's mother was obviously feeling anxious and the remark slipped out. Unfortunately, this sort of critical comment can only increase the trouble because it 'feeds' and strengthens the eating disorder thoughts. Susan, feeling deeply misunderstood, was filled with an urge to escape the room, and skip her meal. In this case she managed to quell the eating disorder bully or voice, which was telling her she would feel better if she ate nothing, but it is important to ensure that this escalating cycle doesn't start.

Avoid criticism as much as possible because it leads only to revenge or despair. If you don't like certain behaviours, try to broach these with your child in a matter-of-fact way. Describe the behaviour you are unhappy about, taking care that your words do not appear attacking or insulting. The confrontation may be easier if you level your complaints at the anorexic 'bully'. Identifying the behaviours of the illness will help you see that your child is really not meaning to behave this way. Label those behaviours as belonging to the bully and make an effort to collaborate with the 'normal' and true part of your child.

Don't drown in despair

As a family you have to come to terms with feelings of loss when your child has anorexia nervosa. You will feel you have lost the child you once had. A common complaint is that before the anorexia nervosa struck the child was as good as gold, perfect in many ways, but after the illness they became rebellious, stubborn and difficult to cope with. You may also have to deal with the loss of your hopes and ambitions for your child. Often, both career and steps towards independence are interrupted. Sometimes these losses can hit the family so badly that overt depression occurs. Your child may become depressed because of the effects of starvation and the narrowed life that results from anorexia nervosa. You, as parents, may become depressed because the burden of caring for someone with anorexia nervosa is so great.

Hold your head up high: shake off shame

Another aspect of the illness is the accompanying stigma. Even in the most forward-looking of communities, psychological illness carries shame. Anorexia nervosa is highly visible. Any passing person will notice your child's skeletal appearance. You may find yourself feeling guilty and ashamed, and that you are to blame. The more you can share your problem with others who understand, the more likely you are to find ways to help. It is no use trying to be an ostrich as the problem is plain to see. Some people, however, are reluctant to accept help; they fear that if they use mental health services, it will go on their record and will be a blot for life. If you are becoming emotionally drained or frazzled, take steps to ensure that you get help. You may need to ask your general practitioner how they can assist. You may want to attend a carers' group (see Chapter 18 for links, including Beat: www.b-eat.co.uk).

Limit setting

Setting limits is necessary in every case of anorexia nervosa. However, the difficulty is that the illness usually occurs during adolescence when there would normally be a gradual stretching and changing of limits to fit with your child's maturation. Parents of a child with anorexia nervosa may receive conflicting advice, which adds to the family's difficulties. Sometimes you are told that you must take total charge of what your child eats. Others advise that there is nothing you can do to control your child's eating, and that the child must decide what to do. If the child hits rock bottom in the process, so be it. As a parent, you might find yourself vacillating between no limits and unreasonable demands. The solution is to set limits that you believe in and are willing to defend if they are tested. We cannot tell you what these limits are. The exact boundaries of the limits are not as important as the fact that you, as parents, have agreed on them.

Limits are specified in specialised eating disorders units. For example, when working with an outpatient, we have a limit of under-nutrition, below which we will not work. If the patient continues to lose weight or fails to gain weight, we will ensure that they are admitted to hospital. In hospital, the limits are different. In a professional unit, the limit will be a weight gain of a fixed amount, for example, 1kg each week.

Think carefully about what limits to adopt and what action you will take if your child breaks them. The limits need to be reasonable and capable of implementation. You will have to stand your ground in confronting the illness despite persuasion, demands or threats. Be determined not to give in. Otherwise, the illness bully will strengthen its hold, and we don't want that.

Problem solving

Families with a sufferer of anorexia nervosa have at least one problem: their child is not eating enough to maintain a normal weight. Commonly, there are other problems too. These may or may not relate to other aspects of the anorexia nervosa. If you as a family encounter a problem, there are three basic strategies to help you deal with it:

1.   Change the situation so you can overcome the problem:

    a)   adjust both desired and actual goals to a compromise position; or

    b)   alter your perception of the situation so it is no longer a problem.

2.   Readjust goals so they are consistent with the present.

For example, with anorexia nervosa in the family, you can decide if you want to work towards your child regaining health. However, if your child has been ill for 30 years despite many attempts at treatment, you may decide to accept that your child will remain disabled by their illness but you will do all you can to help them make their life as comfortable and safe as possible. Or you might work towards a compromise solution in which you help your child maintain their weight above the crisis level but you don't nag them with expectations of grandchildren or even a job. The following example illustrates how one family learned to cope better with their child's anorexia nervosa.

Julia

Julia, aged 24, developed anorexia nervosa when she was away at university. Her tutors, noticing her declining health, would not let her continue her course. Eventually she returned home to live with her parents. They were very worried and did all they could to help. However, if they tried to help with a meal, Julia became rebellious, stormed off and refused to eat anything. Julia's mother took all the setbacks and fluctuations in Julia's eating and weight personally and this worrying brought on migraines.

Arriving home from work at the end of a long day, her husband was doubly irritated and upset to find his wife ill in bed in a darkened room and no end in sight with his adult child's continuing anorexia. The parents discussed this problem together.

They decided that unlike many other problems that they had faced in their family life, this was one they couldn't solve practically. As their child was attending a specialist clinic, they decided to ease their involvement in the small details of the illness. They understood from the specialist that Julia could take five or more years to heal from her anorexia and regain her sense of self. By taking a longer-term view and developing a new perspective, they eased the pressure of expecting too much too soon.

Problems are a fact of life and we have to accept them and their effect on us. A perfect solution may not be available but there are often effective options. Patience helps in detecting the best way forward.

Understanding the problem. If you have a problem, it needs to be clearly defined. Gather as many facts and as much information about the problem as you can find. Take a Sherlock Holmes approach: who, what, when, where, why and how? List and describe these facts with detachment as though they are to be presented on a news bulletin. Be as specific as possible. What elements of the situation make it a problem? Sometimes assumptions or premature judgements can turn an event into a problem. Get everyone's views on the difficulty, especially your child's.

Generating solutions. Once the problem is defined, the next step is to think of as many solutions as possible. Keep a written list so that you do not forget any. If you come up with some really wacky ideas, write them down, too, as sometimes these contain an element of truth or can spark many new ideas. Allow this brainstorming phase to take place as creatively as possible. Do not prematurely criticise any of the solutions. This is a hard task for families with a member suffering from anorexia nervosa, as high standards often abound. Remember that the aim of this exercise is to produce as many, practical or impractical, solutions as possible. Put your critical hat on later. Right now you want quantity, not quality.

Choosing a solution. Now you have a list of solutions, the next stage is to choose the best option. Writing down the pros and cons of each one can be helpful. You may need to compromise or plan to try one out with the proviso that you will later try another if this one fails. When you have selected your solution, make sure the family agrees about how to implement it. What is the first step? Does anyone see any blocks that will prevent this taking place? Make sure everyone understands who is to do what. Writing down the roles is a good idea so that you all can agree on what has been said.

Review. Set aside time to review progress. Were any of the steps involved in finding the solution too difficult to carry out? Are further skills or resources needed? Is it time to go back and choose a different solution or does it make more sense to persevere and find ways round this roadblock? If the solution has worked, sit back and congratulate yourselves. Go out and give yourselves a family treat.

Here is how Charlotte and her family tackled her problem.

Charlotte

Charlotte was 16. She had been vegetarian for four years. At 15, she had had an operation on her hip. Complications occurred and another two operations were required. Charlotte was in hospital for several months and her weight gradually fell over this period. Charlotte was delighted, as she considered herself and her family rather overweight. She had been teased since she was 11, just prior to puberty when she had some puppy fat. Two months before her operation she became vegan and when she returned home her weight continued to fall. Her parents felt concerned as she had lost a lot of weight, had not had a period for nine months and was preoccupied by counting calories and reading cookery books. Charlotte denied she had a problem, and was determined not to gain weight. 'I refuse to be a fat person,' she said. But her parents were equally resolved in wanting to tackle her diet. They sat down with Charlotte and produced the following ideas:

1. Force Charlotte to give up a vegan diet and make her eat what the rest of the family were eating.
2. Put the whole family on a vegan diet and insist that Charlotte eat with them.
3. Come to a compromise and ask Charlotte to return to being vegetarian until her growth and development had finished and she had given the operations on her hip time to heal. (After such an operation bone remodelling might take up to two years.)
4. Go with her to a specialist dietician with expertise in vegan diets.
5. Allow Charlotte to stay on a vegan diet but ensure that she had protein, oil and mineral supplements.

When they had drawn up this list of options, the family considered the pros and cons of each one. They decided to go for the fourth option. Father was given the job of implementing this. He contacted the dietician's professional organisation for a list of names. Charlotte and her family decided to judge the usefulness of this step by monitoring her weight. They agreed that her weight should increase by half a kilogram each week. If, after six weeks, no progress was made they would consider trying one of the other options.

After the visit to the dietician, Charlotte added 115–170g of nuts to her diet each day. Her weight slowly increased to be in the normal range. After six months, her periods returned.

When your partner has anorexia nervosa

Although many of the things we describe for children apply equally well to adults, there are some differences if your partner has anorexia.

You most probably will have found that your partner's illness has affected your life in many ways. Like anyone who lives with a sufferer, you need to look after your own wellbeing. If you have children, you may need to give them extra attention, as your partner may be too ill to look after them as they might wish.

Here are some basic aims that you may want to try to keep in mind:

1. Maintain a balance of power between you. (It's easy to give in to the demands of the anorexic bully.)
2. Aim to increase or focus on the aspects of the relationship that give you pleasure.
3. Ensure that you both have time off. Let your spouse or partner have time off from care-giving.

4. Look after your own wellbeing. Get support from a trusted friend or mother- or father-in-law.

The sexual side of your relationship probably will have suffered. It is important not to assume that a sexual relationship will resume immediately on weight gain. Re-engagement in life, and all it has to offer, often takes time. You may need to rebuild your relationship by doing the things you enjoyed when you first met. After a long period of illness, we often find that both partners may need some help rebuilding their sexual life.

13 Confronting the eating challenge

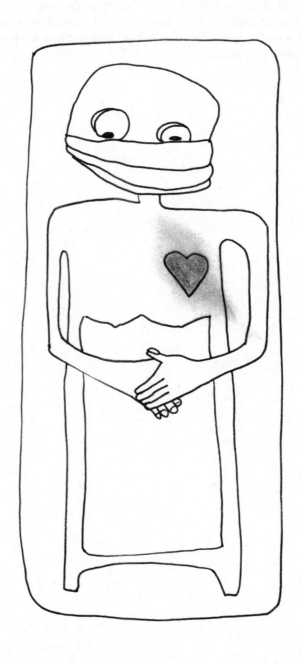

Prescribing what families should do to help with re-feeding a sufferer depends on the eating disorder's development and level of risk.

The family of an adult sufferer can help by providing information, resources and feedback that facilitate the move into recovery. Family members can assist recovery by providing support and guidance, and an emotional buffer against the eating disorder bully.

However, younger sufferers may not be at the developmental stage to grapple with the complex abstract psychological processing and understanding needed to withstand the pull of the anorexic bully. Parents therefore have to step in and guide their child into action. This may also apply to carers of adult patients if insight into the severity of the illness is lost. There are no strict chronological cut-off points – each set of parents, each partner must make their own decision.

Stages of treatment

Treatment of anorexia nervosa usually has three parts:

1. The restoration of a healthy weight to prevent dangerous physical problems.
2. Helping the sufferer recognise and combat anorexic attitudes.
3. Understanding the personality features and environmental difficulties that may have increased the risk of developing an eating problem.

Treatment does not necessarily take place in this sequence. Early intervention is important because, once the illness sets in, many other problems emerge.

Families who have a young child with anorexia nervosa need to be more actively involved in addressing and overcoming the anorexic behaviour. For example, parents need to supervise meals and prevent compulsions taking control. This is hard but vital work. One advantage is that links with friends, school and other areas of life are easier to maintain. An advantage of inpatient treatment is that in specialist units other sufferers can give help and support. Problems can be shared, reducing isolation and alienation. Importantly, a supportive environment also can be created in the home by joining a parent support organisation (see Chapter 18 for links to local and online self-help groups).

Staff rotate on shifts at an eating disorders unit, but at home the parents have the responsibility of confronting the child's illness around the clock. Standing up to the illness 24/7 is crucial in counteracting its sneaky and manipulative ways. Even when fuelled by the power of parental love, the provision of such a high level of constant care can be exhausting and time out is essential to avoid 'burn out'. One difficulty for parents is they cannot treat their child with clinical detachment. Often the parents' level of empathy is so great that they are unable to distinguish the anorexic 'bully' from the normal non-anorexic part of their child. This can render efforts ineffective – and, at worst, they may inadvertently strengthen the illness bully and jeopardise the health of the child. Parents can guard against this risk by empowering themselves with knowledge about the illness. Reading books, collaborating with the treatment team and sharing with other parents will help discern when the anorexia is 'talking' and what behaviour is reasonable.

Food comes first

Low weight adversely affects the mind, and anorexic attitudes cannot be addressed without also tackling life-threatening starvation. Speculating about hidden, underlying reasons as to why the anorexia developed is unhelpful: such diversion may allow the illness to gain an increasingly tighter stranglehold. In Chapter 5 we discuss why many consequences of starvation are self-perpetuating. A primary task, therefore, of a parent or partner of someone suffering from an eating disorder, is to work with the sufferer to find a way of preventing further weight loss.

What do I do about food?

Again this depends in part on the sufferer. They may have reached the stage where they are trying hard to get well and have asked for your help. Alternatively, as a responsible parent, you may need to step in to stop your child compromising their health or social and career development or even putting their life at risk. Do not be frightened to step in even if you fear that your child or partner is too old for you to adopt this role. Remember that insight into the dangers and risks of anorexia nervosa is lost once the condition really takes a hold.

Never let your child or partner convince you that going on a diet will be good for them. Don't buy slimming magazines or low-calorie foods for them or the rest of the family. Stick to a healthy diet of normal foods. Trying to tempt the sufferer to eat with special meals of their favourite foods is a trap that is easy to fall in to. Despite your efforts, they will probably refuse to eat, leaving you feeling rejected and resentful after all your preparation. Similarly, filling the fridge with 'naughty' tempting foods is not helpful. If the sufferer succumbs, their illness will make them feel more mortified than ever.

The journey towards a normal, healthy diet is best taken a step at a time. For the sufferer, reducing their over-controlled behaviour and facing the consequences of weight gain is extremely difficult. Following a carefully calculated, individual plan to produce a predictable, steady gain may be useful (see pages 171–173). A dietician can help with this. Taking the person through the calculations to estimate their individual energy needs can help build their confidence that their weight can behave predictably. Use of standard equations produces a reasonably accurate estimate of how many calories a day need to be eaten to maintain a healthy weight (see Appendix).

To increase the sufferer's variety of food, you will find a series of small changes more useful rather than attempting an immediate move to 'normal'. Small snacks will probably be easier for them to eat than normal-sized meals. The feeling of a bloated, distended stomach is less marked, and the food itself seems less daunting in limited quantities. The sufferer will most likely be able to eat larger amounts of 'safe' foods, while moving more gently towards increased amounts of 'risky' foods. For example, a first step towards oil-based foods may be low-fat spread, semi-skimmed milk, or tuna fish. A first move towards more sugary food may be a muesli bar, or fruit yogurt. For someone who has never eaten breakfast, a glass of orange juice can be a start with toast added later, then maybe cereal. At all times, eating enough to prevent weight loss is vital, and weight gain also is likely to be necessary. But normal eating does not have to resume immediately.

Mealtimes: if your child lives at home with you

Your child may have become very interested in food and want to do the cooking for the family. This is not the good sign it may seem. Explain to them that while they are ill you will not let them cook for the family, as this is part of their anorexic preoccupation with food. You may decide that your child can cook their own meals but stipulate that if they fail to gain weight, you will cook for them. Try to have regular family mealtimes. Let your child know that you would like them to try to eat with you, but don't be surprised if they don't or only manage a very little at first. Try hard to make mealtimes happy and not the focus of family conflict. Food is already a terrifying issue for your child and fighting about it will only make it more so. Talk about the good things that have been happening during the day. Discuss a favourite meal or book. Anything but food.

Problems

A common occurrence is for feelings of hunger to reappear with a vengeance once a pattern of eating re-emerges. This is very frightening for the sufferer – their worst nightmare come true. They fear that they will become bulimic, that they will never be able to stop eating and will blow up like a balloon. This is a normal phase. It does not mean that the sufferer will develop bulimia nervosa, although some do. Men who were starved as part of an experiment in the 1950s went through a phase of binge eating when they were allowed access to more food. Victims of famine binge eat when food arrives. Out-of-control overeating develops as a result of weight loss and, of course, in anorexia nervosa, by definition, weight loss is large. If the so-called binges are analysed, they are often not that big and the daily intake including the contents of the binge is often well below the recommended calorie level.

We can understand why this pattern develops as it represents one of the body's feedback control mechanisms. The body acts as if it has a lipostat, that is, a monitor that can detect how much fat tissue there is in the body. Fat tissue secretes a protein, which acts on the brain to control appetite and metabolism. If the amount of fat tissue is low, little of this 'satiety' protein is produced. This leads to increased appetite. Conversely, once the fat tissue reaches normal levels, higher amounts of this 'satiety' protein are secreted and appetite falls.

The amount of this 'satiety' protein produced therefore depends on the genetic make-up and on the state of nutrition (i.e. the size of fat stores). Many questions remain, including the way in which anorexia nervosa overrides this feedback mechanism.

We are certain of some facts. People at risk of anorexia nervosa do not appear to have the obesity gene, that is, they are able to produce normal levels of the 'satiety' protein. Commonly, the families of sufferers with anorexia nervosa tend towards leanness rather than obesity. Body composition returns to a lean/normal size after recovery from anorexia nervosa. Anorexia nervosa does not lead to obesity.

Therefore, the increased hunger that occurs during weight recovery is a temporary and normal phase. It will gradually pass if small regular meals are eaten throughout the day and no metabolic 'surprises' are caused by vomiting, fasting and feasting. Bulimia need not become a habit.

The appetite centre of the brain can heal with regularly spaced meals ideally with foods with a low glycaemic index so that blood sugar levels do not swing too much. Ideally it is helpful to not be exposed to highly processed palatable foods that can stoke up addictive processes. Monitoring binges and eating patterns enables the brain's control system to switch into action.

Involvement in eating

Level of involvement in re-feeding will depend on the development stage of the sufferer and also whether the level of starvation is so severe that the capacity for rational thought is lost. There are many ways of ensuring that the sufferer has a regular eating pattern. The most effective way is for parents or a partner to sit with the sufferer while the meal is eaten. You will need to encourage them when eating becomes difficult. This may take the form of talking through every mouthful. For example, 'That's right, now take another forkful, in it goes. Now, another.' If this degree of supervision is needed, one-to-one interaction may be called for.

If the sufferer takes a very long time to eat, you may have to set aside an hour or more to sit with them during the meal. Don't give up or the illness will be strengthened. Plan a distraction, like doing a word puzzle, or reading a favourite book out loud, while the meal is being eaten, and plan an enjoyable event afterwards, such as a walk together, if the meal is eaten in the allotted time. Whatever plan you adopt, remember to have regular meetings to review progress and plan further strategies.

One option is to use high-calorie drinks from the chemist or from your general practitioner if eating become too slow or difficult.

Clare's parents decided to adopt this approach after she had spent three to four hours on each meal. They explained their decision in this way: 'We know how difficult it is for you to eat, but we are not going to stand by and see you destroy your life and your health. We want you to drink up these supplements as food is too difficult at the moment.'

Once you have set these limits you must stick with them. Adopting this role will be uncomfortable, but reassure yourself that you are standing up to the illness on behalf of your loved one. It is no different to administering unpleasant anticancer drugs that are likely to make them feel sick and lose their hair in the short term but will save their life. In fact the position is easier than this because, although there is some discomfort with re-feeding, and often the illness will kick up a huge fuss, quite rapidly you will see your child's or partner's hair, skin and circulation improve.

As they gain weight, you may need to reassure them that the food will not make them fat but will be converted to healthy muscle and bone. Discussing the benefits of being a healthy weight again may also help. You may find yourself constantly repeating phrases such as: 'You are not getting fat. You need to eat to make your bones stronger.'

You may decide to ban talk about weight or shape but you will need to use constant reminders to enforce this: 'I think that it is your anorexia illness talking. We agreed that I would not converse with its thoughts, as they are destructive and illogical. Let's discuss issues that are of relevance to your normal true self.'

Isobel

Isobel started to lose weight when she was aged 11 following a change in school. Isobel's mother sat with her and encouraged her daughter to eat slowly. She found it was essential to keep talking in a gentle way. If she saw that her daughter was stopping she would say, 'I know that you to find eating very difficult, and that the anorexia is trying to make you afraid, but it is important for you to eat so your normal self recovers its health. Keep on eating to sustain the part of you that I love and want to grow and develop.' Isobel and her mother used the time spent over meals as an opportunity to discuss the events of the day. Her mother would recount tales of Isobel's life from the day she was born, events during her childhood and also about events from her own life. In this way the protracted mealtimes passed reasonably smoothly. Isobel's mother made sure that during this time she was not distracted by her other children or household tasks. She arranged for her mother to come in and feed the other children and supervise their homework, and on some days her husband would come and take the other children away. She put the telephone on to the answering machine.

Barbara's family adopted another approach.

Barbara

Barbara was 22 when she developed anorexia nervosa and was living away from home. However, when her anorexia had been present for three years and was interfering with her career and social life, she decided to return home so that she could get her parents' care and support. She preferred this option to going into hospital. She and her parents decided to let her be totally independent about her meals. She went to the shops and bought food for herself. She ate her food in the dining room alone. Her parents agreed that they would not enquire about her food intake other than to ask her whether she was making progress in terms of weight. She arranged to go to her general practitioner each week where the practice nurse recorded her weight. She let her parents know that she was making progress. Gradually, she was able to eat meals with the family.

It is helpful to have an outside reference point to establish whether the work you are doing at home is progressing or whether a new solution is needed. Being weighed regularly by a neutral party such as a practice nurse is often helpful.

Other families have come up with other solutions.

Jane
Jane and her parents found that mealtimes became very tense and defusing this was difficult. Their solution was for Jane to go each evening to her grandmother's and eat her meal there. Her grandmother, who understood the need for constant vigilance and support, had more time and was able to be more relaxed, and Jane felt it easier to eat in these surroundings.

The correct amount to eat

In hospitals, because of the need to avoid prolonged in patient treatment, the weight gain range is usually 1 to 2 kilograms per week. At home such a large goal is not necessary and the weight gain rate can be negotiated. To gain a kilogram (2.2 pounds) in weight, approximately an extra 7000kcal over and above the basal level needs to be eaten. What does this mean? The resting metabolic requirements are about 2000kcal a day, so if you want to gain a kilogram (2.2 pounds) a week you need to eat 3000kcal a day. This means a normal amount of food plus half again. If the goal is to gain 0.5 kg (1.1 pounds a week), you need to eat an extra 500 calories, 2500kcal per day to gain weight at this steady rate. It often comes as quite a surprise to realise how much needs to be eaten to gain weight.

The increased calorie intake can be added as snacks – for example, a sandwich at 11am and 3pm and a banana before going to bed at night. Other families may opt for food supplements such as Ensure, Complan or meal replacements. Ready-made meals and pre-packed snacks can eliminate deliberations about what food to give to your child or partner.

Food choices

If the level of starvation is severe, low roughage food is sensible. This is because muscle has been lost from the gut wall and it may be difficult for the gut to cope with too much bulk. At this stage, do not worry if the diet is repetitive. For example, a baked potato and cottage cheese three times a day is acceptable. It is best to stick to a routine and gradually introduce new foods, as too much novelty will cause the sufferer to feel guilty and overly fearful.

Do not be bullied or bamboozled. Many carers say, 'Yes, but you should see the amount she eats, it's more than I do.' Whatever you do, never say anything like this in front of your child or partner, because you will trigger immediate guilt, and empower the illness. Commonly, people with anorexia nervosa eat large amounts of low-calorie foods, such as vegetables and salads. Do not be sidetracked by the sight of such foods piled on a plate. Insist that food of an adequate calorie density is eaten. Some high-quality protein foods, such as fish, are necessary. Choose fish that decreases the risk of heart disease (e.g. sardines, mackerel, tuna and salmon). A good guide for foods with the correct balance for growth and recovery are seed foods (e.g. bananas, avocados, beans and nuts).

Don't get bullied into providing a fat-free diet. Some oils are essential for good health. They are especially critical for cell growth. Health warnings about fats may be appropriate for overweight middle-aged men but not for people with anorexia. Cholesterol levels are high in the starvation state of anorexia nervosa (see Chapter 6) but return to normal after weight gain. Point out this paradox if you are challenged with a 'healthy eating' argument.

Below is an example of a diet plan. This is unlikely to be a suitable first goal. You don't need an expert dietician to tell you what meals to serve. There is nothing subtle and complex about the dietary requirements. Simply, you need adequate calories, that is, a dietary intake of more than 2000 calories each day.

Jane's meal plan

8.15am – Breakfast
Fruit juice
1 small box cereal
200ml skimmed milk
1 slice brown bread
1 pat margarine/butter
1 spoon marmalade
1 pot tea or coffee

10.30am – Mid-morning
Coffee with milk (skimmed)
1 avocado or banana

12.30pm – Lunch
Main course – piece of grilled meat or prepared salad or vegetarian dish
Pudding – yoghurt, fruit salad or fruit

1 cup of tea/coffee
1 cup of water

3.30pm – Mid-afternoon
Tea with skimmed milk
Yogurt or 2 plain savoury biscuits or sandwich

6.30pm – Supper
Main course – same as lunch
Fruit/yogurt
1 cup of water
1 cup of tea with skimmed milk

Bedtime
Hot drink with skimmed milk and banana

It may be easier for the sufferer to initially follow exactly the same diet each day and gradually make exchanges to increase her variety of foods. For example, fish could be switched for the chicken and a pear for an apple.

Louise

Louise had lost weight rapidly and was a vegetarian. She had been eating only fruit for weeks before her diagnosis. She arrived at the clinic literally dragging her foot because the nerves leading to it were not working properly. Also she could not get up from a crouching position.

She embarked on this meal plan:

Breakfast
Glass skimmed milk
2 oatcakes spread with smooth peanut butter
Apple

10.30am – Snack
Coffee made with skimmed milk
2 oatcakes spread with peanut butter
Banana

12.30pm – Lunch
Baked potato with cottage cheese
Fromage frais

3.30pm – Snack
Milky coffee or milkshake made with skimmed milk and frozen fruit
2 oatcakes spread with peanut butter

Supper
Baked potato with cottage cheese
Fromage frais

Snack
Milky drink
Banana

This diet is high in calcium, which helps to restore nerve and muscle function.

Susan

Susan found that if she went to her supermarket and bought ready-made meals she felt secure in that she didn't have to weigh her food or feel anxious about having the exact number of calories. She was able to supplement two meals from this with snacks, such as a peanut butter sandwich and a glass of milk, which she kept constant.

Here is her diet plan:

Breakfast
Milky coffee
2 Weetabix with milk

Snack
Crunch bar
Milky drink

Lunch
Prepared meal
Yoghurt

Snack
Pack of nuts and raisins
Milky drink

Supper
Prepared meal
Yogurt

Snack
Piece of fruitcake
Yoghurt drink

You can probably think of many other sorts of snacks. Your list might include a peanut butter sandwich, a packet of fruit and nuts, an avocado, a crunch bar or a bowl of cereal.

Changing weight control measures

Laxatives

Take care not to get involved in purging behaviour. Never buy laxatives for a person with an eating disorder or give them money to buy them. If you do this, it suggests that you approve of this behaviour, which belongs to the eating disorder bully. Explain that constipation and slow gut function treated with laxatives can be physically harmful. Explain that you care about them and therefore will not contribute to the self-harm tendencies that are part of their illness. Explain that you love them, are there for them and are determined to help confront the illness, and be by their side all the way to recovery and beyond.

Vomiting

If you suspect that vomiting is taking place, don't pretend that it isn't happening; state your reasons for concern factually but refrain from expressing disgust or being critical. Let them know that you realise how upsetting this is for them and how guilty they may feel. Remember that emotional blackmail never helps; so don't try to make the sufferer feel guilty about upsetting you. Just point out the damage they are doing to their health. Offer to help them combat the urge to vomit, perhaps by quietly sitting holding hands after meals even if this takes two hours or more. A diversion such as watching television or another mutually pleasant pastime can help ease the feelings of anxiety.

The setting of rules without the consent of the sufferer is unhelpful. You may encounter and encourage only deception, mistrust and manipulation. The aim in your negotiations must be to listen to their concerns and ensure that they are aware of the reasons for your worries. For example, explain that you are concerned because they are putting their life at risk and may cause long-term problems to their health. Try to find a chink in their armour of indifference to the consequences so that you can work together. Set goals that are realistic. It is inappropriate and unhelpful to say: 'You must not vomit again.' This is too high a target and will lead to failure and relapse.

Rosemary
Rosemary was very underweight and also vomited frequently. Her mother voiced her anxiety to Rosemary this way:

> Your father and I are very concerned about your health. We know that you also recognise some difficulties. You have told me how, on occasions, you feel extremely tired. Going out with your friends is now too much of an effort. I think these problems result from your anorexia and vomiting. We would like you to have a better quality of life. We would like to help. Our suggestions include: the possibility for me to stay with you for three hours after each meal. Another possibility would be for us to lock the bathroom door. Alternatively, you could promise us that you will delay your vomiting by at least an hour after each meal. Can we discuss this further together?

Exercise

Exercise may seem to be healthy but some sufferers use it in an obsessive way to control their weight or anxiety. Over-activity is harmful at low weight because the body's danger signals, which indicate overwork, often may not be noticed or are ignored in people with anorexia nervosa. In other cases, the drive to over-exercise overrides the pain of stress fractures. Patients with anorexia nervosa are at risk of fractures as their bones are very thin. Other sufferers continue to exercise even though they develop friction-induced sores. As the skin is dry and fragile in people with anorexia nervosa, these sores take a long time to heal.

Patricia
Patricia spent the entire day on the go. She would walk for miles, swim for two hours and do step aerobic classes. Her parents expressed concern that she was wearing out her body and that she needed more balance within her life. They therefore agreed to help her set realistic goals. Patricia reduced by one hour each week the amount of time she was walking. She stopped swimming. She continued the aerobics class on three nights per week because it also contained a much-needed social element.

What is an acceptable amount of exercise? When weight loss is severe, no exercise at all is advisable. That's right. None. A reasonable amount of exercise is half an hour three times a week when weight is clear of the anorexic range; that is, above 17.5kg/m^2.

Jane

Jane had lived with anorexia nervosa for 12 years. She became critically ill and was admitted to hospital for tube feeding on several occasions. Her brother returned to live in her hometown after he had been away at university. He suggested that if Jane could keep her weight up after her last admission she would be able to go to the gym with him. Jane became interested in step aerobics, which she started doing twice a week. After three months, holding her weight steady, she began to train as a teacher. Two years later her periods had returned, she was at a normal weight and she gave lessons in step aerobics.

Taking stock

Set aside time on a regular basis to review progress. Weight is a good yardstick to consider if the sufferer is underweight and still losing (however, the anorexic bully can use tactics that make weight unreliable and so you may need help from medical professionals to use more global health markers such as blood tests and physical signs). Don't let yourself get sidetracked into lengthy discussions about uncertain markers of progress. If weight is not increasing, the solutions that you and your child or partner have come up with to gain weight have not been working. Use the tactic of collaborating with the sufferer against the anorexia bully. Don't let yourself get too emotionally aroused, otherwise your ability to think of solutions will be impaired. Don't take failure personally. Remember that the sufferer's behaviours are symptoms of their illness and not a deliberate intention to rebel and be nasty to you.

A ruler of change is a simple device that can help structure these goal-setting conversations. Draw a line with zero at one end (no change) with 10 (fully committed to change) at the other. Ask the sufferer what number they are. People with eating disorders are usually ambivalent about change and therefore rarely score 10. Ask what would have to change to get a score closer to 10. If the score is above zero, reflect on the factors that would allow them to have a higher score.

Ask the sufferer if they know why the solutions have not worked. Can they come up with an alternative? Work with your child or partner to generate a variety of options to consider. For instance:

- Do they require more foods?
- What foods would they like to introduce?
- Do they want more help from anyone?
- Can you invite a relative to stay and devote time to easing the problem?
- Do you need to consider taking time off work?
- Do you need to ask friends to help with other children?
- Do you need to consider hospital admission?

By generating a variety of options, you can both feel that there is an element of choice. It may be necessary to come back to some of the options. So write them down as 'minutes' of your meeting, along with your final decision on the way forward.

People with low self-esteem have a tendency to be over-sensitive to failure, and are unable to recognise success. When this is pointed out, people with an eating disorder will often recognise in themselves a tendency to perfectionism, and to write off their efforts as failure unless they have been totally successful, which, of course, is impossible in many situations. It can help to point out achievements, highlighting progress in treatment. A diary, building up a record over a period of time, is another useful tool. Such a record may also be a source of encouragement to you as you look for signs that your child or partner is improving. As their confidence increases, they can gradually resume responsibility for eating their meals alone.

If the sufferer is not ready to accept help with eating, offer to assist in another way. Some ideas are outlined in the next chapter.

14 Recovery is more than gaining weight

Sufferers from anorexia nervosa have confused views about their bodies. For example, if you comment on the weight gain and improved appearance of someone with anorexia nervosa, you may be shocked at the response. You may think you are doing the right thing by providing reassurance that they are looking 'well', but such a remark is more likely to alarm them by triggering intense eating disorder thoughts. Such thoughts will remind the sufferer that, contrary to what you say, they look awful, that they are fat and greedy for eating so much food. In a bid to ease these acute feelings of guilt, they are likely to vow to exercise more than usual or to not eat for the rest of the day.

Appearance and body image

Commonly, people with eating disorders talk about feeling fat even though they might on some level recognise that they are thin. This helps to explain why eating is difficult: the sufferer feels fat and therefore does not need or deserve food. People with anorexia nervosa often experience 'anosognosia' – they are unaware they are sick; they do not feel ill and perceive their own behaviours and thoughts as normal. This is not a choice or conscious denial, but a feature of their illness and brain dysfunction.

It is unhelpful if there is 'fat talk' in or outside the home. Talk of diets and critical comments about appearance feed the anorexic bully. Avoid family and friends who are on diets and do not have fashion magazines lying around the house.

You may need to help the sufferer become aware of the reality of their thinness. One way is to obtain a current photograph of them. In a warm, supportive environment look at this photo together and contrast it with a picture taken before development of the illness. Alternatively, stand with the sufferer in front of a mirror and, with much reassurance, slowly and calmly look at your reflections. Often, people with anorexia nervosa avoid confrontation with reality. They do not like looking in mirrors. They find this frightening, and have difficulty seeing themselves as others see them.

Another approach is to get some size 16 clothes from a shop where you can try them on at home and return them. Size 16 is the average size of a British woman. Suggest that the sufferer tries on these clothes. Ask her what she makes of it? Is she bigger than average?

Other ways of helping body image problems may be to question our present cultural stereotypes. Rosemary's mother took her to Hampton Court where they toured the house and looked at the portraits. Rosemary was interested to notice that all the women in the portraits looked rather plump by today's standards. This insight enabled her to contemplate the possibility that modern standards are really reflections of fashion and that, due to photo-refining techniques, current media images are often illusions.

Social events

Social events can be difficult for people with anorexia nervosa and this can be an aspect of support that siblings and friends are in the best position to provide. Often, sufferers have missed out on the normal adolescent stages of social development because of their illness. Start with an event that is relatively non-threatening. Remember you cannot force socialisation and that too much pressure can be counterproductive. Stick to gentle encouragement. If your partner has anorexia nervosa, be sure to maintain your own social life – otherwise you will feel isolated, too. As a parent, it may seem inappropriate to be arranging an older child's social life. However, you help create opportunities by arranging for long time friends to call in and perhaps participate in family outings.

Martina
Martina's parents were aware that she had become isolated from her friends. They made arrangements to leave the house on Saturday evenings and encouraged Martina to invite one or two friends around to watch a film with her and have a snack.

Obsessions and compulsions

Sufferers with anorexia nervosa often have marked obsessive–compulsive problems that may have developed before the illness but are more pronounced when ill. Aside from their 'obsessive' concern about body weight, size and shape, many have obsessions about such matters as cleanliness, tidiness, contamination, danger and harm to others. They can also have compulsive rituals such as excessive hand washing, repeated checking, counting and doing things in a certain way. They may ask repeatedly for reassurance from people who are close to them, such as 'Did I do it all right?' or 'Is it OK if I do not check that again?'

It is important that you do not fall into the trap, which is all too easy, of saying 'Yes' or 'OK'. Such responses do not provide reassurance, and perpetuate the cycle. You are likely to be asked: 'Are you sure I did it OK?' or 'Do you really mean that?' Rather than answer such questions, you will help the recovery process more by saying something like: 'I do not agree with your obsessional rituals and will make no comment on them.' Or, if this seems too tough, say that you will provide reassurance with limits that will gradually be reduced. This will not be easy but remember discomfort now will lead to future improvement.

Mary
Mary, an 18-year-old girl who had anorexia and was treated in hospital, did everything in fours. She felt she 'had to do this'. For example, when she got out of bed in the morning, she would make her bed four times. She would enter any room, including the bathroom, only at the fourth attempt, having

gone in and come out three times. She was obsessed with the idea that, if she did not do everything in fours, some great harm would come to her family and to herself. She had these problems almost as long as she had the eating difficulties.

Obsessive–compulsive problems usually worsen when the eating problem is severe, and the intensity eases with better health. Sometimes, special treatment may be needed. There are things that you can do to help someone with this additional problem. You can encourage the sufferer to try to refrain from the compulsive rituals. Give a clear instruction, and then stand firm. For example: 'I want you to get dressed now. I will not respond or reassure you when your obsessional side tries to engage me in the obsession/anxiety/reassurance circle.' You will feel discomfort but this will settle. Spending time with the sufferer at times when the rituals are most likely to occur is useful. They can refrain from them with your help and support. Remember, though, that prolonged reassurance makes the situation worse. If the sufferer repeatedly seeks your reassurance, respond with something like: 'Do you remember, we agreed not to talk about it?'

Do not be alarmed by the appearance of obsessive–compulsive problems in your daughter or partner. They do not indicate anything sinister and can be dealt with relatively easily in many cases. Treatments for severe obsessive–compulsive problems are quite effective.

Depression

Low mood and depression are consequences of starvation, whether they result from famine or are produced experimentally. Several men in the Ancel Keys (1950) experiment in Minnesota became very depressed when they lost weight. One or two became so severely depressed that they were admitted to hospital.

Many of the depressive symptoms seen in people with anorexia nervosa resemble those in patients with a depressive illness. Thinking and emotions change. Sufferers become sad. They are unable to derive pleasure in the ways they would have previously. Concentration is impaired. Locked in their illness, they are unable to contemplate, let alone look forward to, the future.

Distinguishing the physical features of depression from those of starvation is difficult. Poor sleep, fatigue, and physical aches and pains are common to both.

The depression of starvation does not respond easily to antidepressant drugs. Such medication appears to be ineffective at very low weight. The best medicine is food, for weight gain alone corrects the depression of starvation. In some cases, depression as a form of mental illness and depression as a symptom of starvation coexist. In this instance, antidepressants are necessary.

Anxiety

High levels of anxiety run in the families of people with eating disorders. Anxiety, caused by sensitivity to threat and fear of other people, or social phobia is most common in anorexia nervosa and can develop early in life. This is associated with vigilance to signs of criticism or anger. Training in attention to kindness and compassion may alleviate this brain bias. One way to do this is for others to keep calm. This is not easy as the biological sensitivity to threat runs in families and eating disorder symptoms provoke profound fear. Therefore, an anxiety spiral can develop within the home like a forest fire. One way to interrupt this symptom escalation is to look after yourself. Allow yourself time out and support to replenish your ability to nurture.

Maintaining employment

Anorexia nervosa has a variety of effects on the workplace. In severe cases sufferers may have to take sick leave because they lack the energy, concentration and stamina necessary to do their job adequately and safely. In such cases, the sufferer may need to negotiate a gradual transition back to work.

The loss of income may cause the sufferer to experience financial difficulties. Parents who pick up the tab and protect their adult child from this hardship may not help the individual to face the reality of their situation.

Conclusion

You will have seen from this chapter that there are no hard and fast rules about what you should do as a parent. The best that you can do is to apply and practise the skills of patience and perseverance. Keep calm and carry on. Aim to be available as a source of support but also be sure to look after yourself.

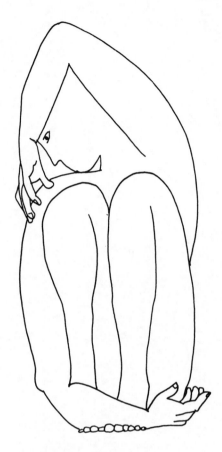

Take good care of yourself

On average, anorexia nervosa lasts about five years. However, about one in four sufferers have an illness that lasts more than ten years and may remain chronic.

Section Four

Guidelines for professionals

15 Guidelines for therapists and carers

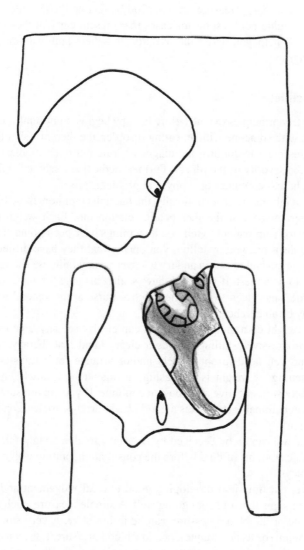

A key feature of anorexia nervosa is that the sufferer doesn't think they have a problem. In the past, this has been termed 'denial'; now it is known as the 'pre-contemplation' stage of the process of change. The person with anorexia nervosa is often blithely unconcerned as they become sicker and sicker while everyone around them frets and panics and gets sucked into the anorexia orbit.

This book is designed to be a resource for sufferers of anorexia nervosa at all stages of motivation. It is also useful for carers and therapists. (The skills and knowledge that you need to deal with more complex cases are covered more comprehensively in *Skills-Based Learning for Caring for a Loved One with an Eating Disorder*, Treasure et al., 2007). Trained counsellors will find this recovery guide book useful for cases that present early in the course of the illness. It will help you assist the sufferer and their family through some of the early stages.

First principles

There are a few principles to note before therapy begins. Importantly, before starting to work with someone with an eating disorder, the therapist should arrange a medical assessment to confirm the diagnosis, rule out other medical conditions and assess the severity of the illness. Further medical assessments will be necessary if weight loss continues or if physical problems arise.

Regular weigh-ins are crucial. Ideally, the therapist monitors these because they are an important part of the therapeutic relationship. Each weigh-in provides opportunity for your patient to tell you how things have been going. They may be reluctant to displease you by telling you openly that they have difficulties. They may fear criticism and rejection and try to cover up any failings. The weight scales allow them to be honest. If you don't have scales, arrange for an accurate weight to be recorded and given to you. The practice nurse at the general practitioner's surgery may be able to help.

Plot the weight on a graph so that you can clearly see any time trends. If the weight is progressively falling, this is a clear signal that therapy is not being effective and you need to obtain help and/or arrange for a transfer to a more specialist setting. If weight is increasing, no matter how slowly, this is a sign that your therapy is effective and you can continue. If you are not sure what to try next and weight remains static, it is a good idea to arrange for a second opinion or a consultation.

Of course, we can all be deceived by measures to alter weight falsely, such as drinking large amounts of fluid before the consultation, putting weights in clothes and other ploys.

Therefore, put time into developing good clinical judgement and be alert to symptoms or signs that all is not going well. A simple measure, such as checking the pulse rate or the blood pressure, can be informative. A very slow heart rate, less than 55bpm (beats per minute), or a low blood pressure, less than 85/60mmttg (millimetres of mercury), is cause for concern. Remember that anorexia nervosa has a mortality level twice that of any other illness and so you must make sure your procedure is safe. Do not be afraid to ask for help.

Expressing and acknowledging your concern and your need to involve others is good practice and will help to model appropriate behaviour for your patient. One of the key maladaptive coping behaviours in anorexia nervosa is that sufferers avoid facing their problems and do not open up to others. Do not be drawn into this pattern of behaviour. The following danger signs indicate that starvation has reached a critical level and that medical help is required urgently:

1. Thigh and shoulder weakness, which makes climbing stairs or brushing hair difficult.
2. Faints or dizziness on getting up suddenly.
3. Fits (episodes when consciousness is lost associated with muscle-jerking).
4. Episodes of light-headedness or panic, with palpitations.
5. Measles-like rash on the skin.
6. Breathlessness.
7. Severe exhaustion.
8. Extremely cold and blue toes.

These signs are markers that indicate that starvation is severe. They must not be ignored. Weight loss of this degree of severity usually requires urgent hospital admission. There also may be more 'silent' dangers, which are only revealed by blood tests. Any 'funny turns' in anorexia nervosa need to be taken seriously as they may be the signals of later serious problems.

You can test muscle power by asking your patient to crouch down on her haunches. Can she rise from this position without using her arms for leverage? If not, this is a sign that muscle function is severely impaired. You must arrange an urgent assessment with a view to immediate admission. Check toes, fingers and nose to assess the state of the circulation. Cold, blue mottling indicates that the peripheral circulation is poor.

Choosing a management plan

How you manage the case will depend on your patient's age and the age at which their anorexia has developed. Obviously the family of the younger patient needs to be included in sessions as they are automatically involved in treating the illness. Also, if the illness developed early in life, and your patient is still living at home, in many ways they will be functioning at the age level at which the anorexia began. Their maturation will be stunted. For example, if the illness began at the age of 11, the sufferer may remain pre-pubertal physically and their mental development also will remain childlike in terms of abstract concepts. Although they may now be aged 24, family support in managing their illness remains important. Research has found that family education and counselling is an effective way to manage symptoms and overcome the effects of the illness.

The family may feel frightened, guilty and confused as to what to do. Use this book as a resource to give them information. They may find it helpful to go over Chapters 2 and 3 so that they can understand what the illness is about and what experiences have contributed to its development.

As we have noted, anorexia nervosa has a long duration, five years on average. Living at close quarters with this problem can cause anxiety and frustration. Emotions such as anger and criticism or the converse, coolness and distancing, can arise. Unfortunately these emotions and behaviours only serve to strengthen and 'feed' the illness. As a therapist, the fostering of a warm, caring relationship within the family can be helpful. Try to reframe worries and concerns into positive features. If, despite your best efforts, the family remains hostile and critical to the sufferer, you will need to sideline their involvement as much as possible. It may be helpful to suggest that the family join a carers' support group. Realising that other families have the same problem and that it is the illness, rather than their child's stubbornness or wilfulness, that is giving them a hard time, can help defuse the tension among parents and other family members. Working through Chapters 11 and 12 may help with this. The only feature that marks families with a sufferer of anorexia nervosa from others is the finding that they are weak on effective problem solving. Therefore, coaching family members in the techniques of problem solving, outlined in Chapter 12, may be useful. Start with simple tasks and gradually guide them upwards.

You will spend more time working with older patients individually. However, collaborative care is to be encouraged. Do not be afraid to recruit members of the family to help when you and the patient think it is necessary, and especially if you are stuck or failing in therapy as evidenced by the weight chart. Working with your patient on the exercises detailed in Chapter 8 can be very important.

Critical points

- Collaborate with a colleague who can give you a medical evaluation before and during your treatment work.
- Weigh your patient regularly.
- Chart the weight and use it as the basis of a collaborative relationship with your patient.
- Communicate regularly with others involved: the general practitioner; the referring agency; members of your team.
- Get help if weight continues to fall.
- Seek a second opinion or consultation if the weight remains static.
- Be alert for medical danger signs and symptoms.
- Involve the family at an age-appropriate level.
- Be sensitive to the demoralisation and frustration that living with a chronic, stigmatising illness can bring.
- Be a resource of information.
- Offer skills training, especially in problem solving, for the family.

16 The family doctor

Making a diagnosis

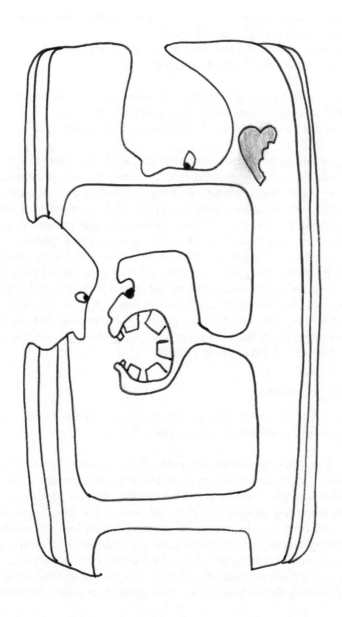

The classical case of anorexia nervosa is not difficult to diagnose. However, eliciting all the symptoms may be a challenge as the sufferer may be unforthcoming. They may have been brought to the clinic reluctantly. They may say they have no worries about their weight loss and that their parents or partner are making a fuss about nothing.

Do not fall into the trap of arguing with the sufferer. Listen to them and then ask questions such as:

- 'Why are your parents worried?' (Or, 'Why is your partner worried?')
- 'What exactly are they worried about?'
- 'Are you able to join in with your friends as easily as before?'
- 'Have you been troubled by feeling the cold?'

Importantly, take the parents' or partners' concerns seriously and do not be fobbed off by the hostile child being somewhat unforthcoming.

You can make the diagnosis if the following criteria are present:

1. *Weight loss* in the absence of organic illness. (If a coherent history of self-induced weight loss is provided, further investigation to rule out other causes of weight reduction is unnecessary.) Atypical presentations do occur in which a vaguely defined abdominal distress is given as an explanation of why eating is difficult. In these cases further investigation may be needed. Failure to grow, rather than a loss of weight, occurs in pre-pubertal children.
2. *Amenorrhoea.* (This may be absent if the patient is taking the contraceptive pill. In males, the equivalent hormonal marker is loss of early morning erections. Obviously, these signs are not present in pre-pubertal children.)
3. *Distorted body image.* Patients may say they feel fat even though they are underweight. (This is not always present. Some patients will say that they know they are thin but they cannot do anything about it.) Also, patients may say they are terrified of gaining weight.

Atypical presentation

Making the diagnosis can be difficult in atypical presentations, such as in sufferers who are younger or older than average, and in males.

- *Children.* Anorexia nervosa occurs in children as young as six years of age. There is a greater proportion of males in the younger age group (young male:female 1:3 vs adolescent M:F 1:10). Children this age may not be able to articulate the reasons why they have lost weight. The diagnosis can be inferred from their behaviour. Reserves of fat are lower in children, and starvation quickly impairs basic physiological function. Peripheral circulatory failure can lead to ischaemic changes in the toes, causing gangrene.
- *Males.* Excessive exercise rather than extreme food restriction may be the way that anorexia nervosa presents in males. Rather than stating that they want to

lose weight, the explanation for the exercise may be that they wish to become fit and build muscle, or do not want to be lazy.

- *Older women*. Women over the age of 30 can develop a syndrome of extreme weight loss with pronounced depressive features. They can usually provide no explanation for their weight reduction, but family members observe that they eat very little. Sufferers deny that they want to be thinner and say they are trying to gain weight. However, their attitude to food and eating is frequently distorted. Often these women have had to face severe stress such as the loss of close family members. Disentangling the features of depression from those of anorexia nervosa can be difficult. However, the depressive features do not respond to antidepressants when patients are at a low weight.

Diabetes

Eating disorders occur more often in people with diabetes. Physical risk is higher with less weight loss – that is, people with diabetes can be ill with a higher BMI – and early specialist treatment is recommended to prevent severe complications.

What can be done in primary care

The practice nurse can be an invaluable source of help and support and can monitor risk and provide guidance for change in combination with self-help tools such as this book. Early intervention is essential to prevent the illness becoming entrenched and so it is vital to observe a low threshold for referral to more specialist care.

17 Guidelines for school staff[1]

Pooky Hesmondhalgh

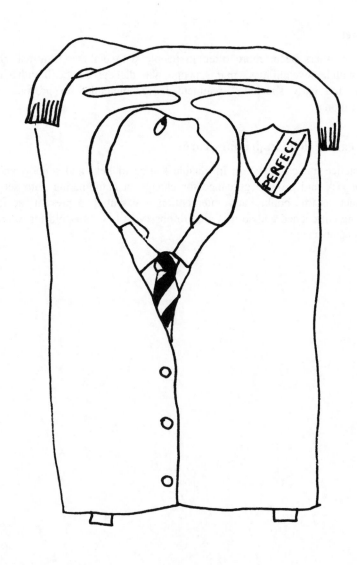

How to support a child with anorexia

School staff often feel unsure about how best to help a pupil with anorexia. They also underestimate how much they can do to help and what a great support they can be. In fact, school staff are well placed to spot the initial warning signs of anorexia, enabling early diagnosis, early intervention and a far better prognosis. Students are often more comfortable talking about food difficulties with a member of school staff than a member of their own family. The school can provide a bridge between the pupil, their family and external care providers to ensure that support is optimal and treatment is effective.

The school also can take practical steps during recovery, including:

* revision of academic expectations
* offering support during mealtimes
* keeping a close eye on weight-related teasing and bullying.

School-specific warning signs that a pupil may be developing anorexia

Some anorexia warning signs are either specific to the school environment or more easily noticed at school. You can look for any of the following.

Weight loss

Rapid or excessive weight loss is a key warning sign that a young person may be developing anorexia. The wearing of several layers of clothes often cleverly hides this weight loss, but PE teachers may notice it very easily when a pupil changes into sportswear or swimwear.

Avoidance of PE or swimming

Pupils may try to find excuses to avoid PE, and swimming in particular. Reasons for this avoidance include fear that the weight loss will become apparent to others; and feelings of embarrassment and shame in changing in front of other people – sufferers of anorexia loathe their body, which they often mistakenly believe to be very fat.

Excessive exercise

However, some pupils spend more time than usual playing sport or using the school gym. This is particularly common in boys with anorexia – they may spend every possible moment working out in the school gym, swimming or running.

Dizziness, tiredness and fainting

Pupils who are not consuming enough calories to sustain themselves throughout the busy school day may appear lethargic during lessons and be prone to dizziness and fainting – especially during PE.

Busy during lunch breaks

A pupil with anorexia is likely to create situations where they are 'too busy to eat' – so keep an eye on the pupil who schedules extracurricular activities for each lunchtime. These pupils may keep themselves busy for two reasons: to provide a distraction from the thought of food and eating, and to help avoid detection. Anorexia nervosa is akin to having a manipulative bully in the mind and therefore a pupil may make use of the ready acceptance in most schools that they do not need to attend the dining hall if they are busy at orchestra practice or similar.

Avoidance of the school cafeteria

As well as keeping themselves busy during lunch, pupils may go out of their way to physically avoid the school cafeteria – or they may act strangely if they cannot avoid being there. They will experience a mixture of fear, panic and disgust and may have panic attacks on entering the cafeteria.

Wearing extra clothing

With little body fat, young people with anorexia often wear extra clothing to keep themselves warm. This is easily noticeable at school as uniforms are harder to adapt than casual clothing. Watch out for the pupil you are constantly having to remind to remove their coat, or who insists on wearing a scarf in class – or who is still wearing a jumper or blazer in summer, long after their classmates have changed into short sleeves.

Perfectionism

Young people with anorexia tend to be perfectionist by nature and this is often exhibited in their schoolwork. They often will stay up until the early hours of the morning perfecting a piece of work, or discard a whole page of writing because they have made a single error. They are likely to be highly disappointed if they achieve anything other than top grades.

Inability to focus in class

As an eating disorder develops and becomes entrenched, it can be very hard for a pupil to focus on their schoolwork. Thoughts of food increasingly dominate their mind and their brain is lacking the energy needed to fuel it. They still set exacting, perfectionist standards for themselves and you may notice their frustration as they struggle to grapple with concepts in class that they may have understood more easily a few months earlier.

Loss of friends

You may notice that a previously popular pupil becomes increasingly socially isolated from friends. As the eating disorder becomes more entrenched, the pupil becomes more obsessed with food and has difficulty thinking of anything else.

When a pupil is causing concern

If you think a pupil may be suffering from anorexia, you should raise your concerns with the person responsible for pastoral care within the school. They may already be aware of the problem, or they may enlist your help in approaching the pupil if you are someone the pupil trusts. If asked to broach the subject with the pupil, you can do this by creating opportunities for the pupil to come to you – at which point your key role is to remain impartial and to listen to them before working with them to decide on the next steps.

Creating opportunities for a pupil to confide in you

A pupil feels more comfortable if they 'make the first move' with regards to talking about their eating disorder as this enables them to feel in control of the situation. To facilitate this you can engineer situations when a pupil can open up to you, perhaps holding them back after class to discuss their homework or similar. Often, a pupil with an eating disorder feels scared and alone, and during the early stages they may welcome the chance to offload to someone. Try to encourage them to broach the subject by asking leading questions such as: 'You don't seem quite yourself lately, how can I help you?' Avoid talking about food or weight directly as this is likely to spook the pupil. Take this first meeting gently and accept that you are unlikely to get to the crux of the issue immediately. Instead, work on building a trusting relationship with the pupil and ensure that they know when and where they can talk to you further about what's on their mind.

Remain calm and don't judge

If a pupil talks to you about their eating difficulties, it's paramount that you remain calm and mask any fear, disgust or worry that you might feel. A huge amount of courage is required for the pupil to open up to you and this is possibly the first time they have admitted their problems, even to themselves. With gentle encouragement, they may allow you to support them. However, a wrong response may cause them to lose confidence in seeking support for their difficulties in you or anyone else.

Don't talk, listen

Allow the pupil to open up and give them as much opportunity to talk as you can. The more they talk about their difficulties, the more they will realise that they need help and support to change eating attitudes and behaviour. You can offer encouragement by asking questions to help them explore how they are feeling, by using open body language and by showing you are listening – for example, by nodding your head and making affirmative sounds.

Confidentiality and talking to parents

If a pupil chooses to confide in you about their eating disorder, they will often ask you to keep the problem a secret. This is not possible as it may jeopardise the pupil's health – and your job. Never promise to keep the problem confidential. Instead, take a proactive approach to sharing the problem in a way that involves the pupil. They will feel more confident about informing other people about their eating disorder if they work with you to decide who should be told, what they should be told, and when. This will help the pupil to feel in control and help you to keep their trust.

Almost always, parents must be told – because they can provide excellent support during recovery and are usually needed for a doctor's referral. Pupils are often reluctant about telling their parents whom they may not want to worry, or whom they may think won't take the problem seriously. Explore these concerns with the pupil – they may like you to be by their side at a face-to-face meeting to inform their parents.

If the pupil discloses that they have a physically, emotionally or sexually abusive relationship with their parents, then you should not inform the parents, but instead bring in the support of skilled professionals such as social services or CAMHs to help you navigate the situation as a matter of urgency.

Working with parents and external agencies

When a pupil is fighting to recover from an eating disorder, they are most likely to succeed if they have consistent support from family, the school and relevant healthcare professionals. The school can provide a link between parents, the pupil and external agencies by arranging and hosting regular meetings. The pupil should attend and form the key focus of these meetings, and everyone involved in their care should look for ways to collaborate. Working together like this can aid and speed effective recovery as the constant, shared vigilance means there is less opportunity for the eating disorder bully to strengthen its hold. Most importantly, the pupil can raise any issues in a safe and supportive environment and everyone can work together to help resolve them.

Academic expectations

These meetings can also provide opportunity to discuss appropriate academic expectations for the pupil. In many cases the school and parents should lower their expectations of the pupil or allow them to defer examinations. The pupil will often strongly resist such changes and there may be room for compromise, but the focus must be on recovery rather than academic results. The school may want to work with the parents to set a reasonable limit on the time that the pupil spends on homework as obsessive, perfectionist traits may see them studying until the early hours of each morning.

Offering support during mealtimes

Mealtimes can be particularly difficult for pupils recovering from anorexia and school staff may wonder how to offer support. Again, you can work with the pupil, their parents and external care agencies involved to determine the best approach – points to consider include:

* where the pupil should eat
* who they should eat with
* what they should eat.

Where to eat

Pupils can often find the school cafeteria daunting – sometimes, during early recovery, a pupil may prefer to return home for meals. If this is practical and the family is happy with this solution, then this can be helpful for a limited period. Alternatively, the pupil can eat their meals elsewhere within the school such as the nurse's office or a quiet classroom, or they may feel more comfortable eating in the cafeteria at a different time to their peers if the lunch system is run in shifts. The ultimate aim is to help the pupil to become comfortable eating with peers in the main dining hall but this may take some time.

Who to eat with

Ensure the pupil is not left to eat alone during recovery. However good their intentions, they are likely to struggle with eating adequate amounts, especially at first. The anorexia bully makes meals a terrifying time and having somebody on hand to offer support can be very helpful. A parent, school nurse or teacher may be a good companion – or a supportive classmate. Again, work towards a point where the pupil is happy eating with their peers but this may need to be accomplished in stages. The pupil also should be accompanied following meals to a) prevent them throwing up what they have eaten and b) to help them quell the panic they may be feeling. Being kept busy chatting with a friend for 20 minutes can help a lot in alleviating feelings of fear and shame.

What to eat

If the care provider has given the pupil a food plan, then this must be followed exactly – to the gram! If no plan has been provided, then discuss with the pupil and the family whether it is better for the school or the parents to provide the meals. Having meals made at home may help the child to feel more in control of what they are eating as they will know exactly what ingredients are in the food. If eating school-made meals, it is helpful to allow the pupil some input into meal choices. If the pupil has to keep a food diary, they should be expected to complete this task, if they can be trusted, but it should be spot-checked for accuracy.

Weight-related bullying and teasing

Your school should take a zero tolerance approach to weight-related bullying and teasing whether or not you have a pupil with anorexia at the school. Pupils who develop eating disorders have often experienced a period of bullying and it is also common for pupils in recovery to suffer a relapse following bullying or teasing. Weight-related teasing of pupils who are recovering from anorexia often comprises seemingly harmless comments or jokes from pupils or teachers. Remember that, especially during early recovery, pupils with anorexia are likely to take to heart, believe, and be terrified by even the most flippant comments about weight or shape.

Note

1   The information in this chapter is based on work supported by the National Institute for Health Research (NIHR) under its programme Grants for Applied Research Scheme (RP-PG-0606-1043). The views expressed herein are those of the author and not necessarily those of the NHS, NIHR or the Department of Health.

18 Where to get support

Eating disorder researchers, therapists, carers, parents and sufferers have contributed their recommendations to this resource list. The list is by no means complete, for new articles, research outcomes and books are emerging constantly. However, it does provide a sound base on which to start your eating disorder research, seek support and gain awareness.

Eating disorder advocacy and support organisations

**Parent-led or focused organisation

International

Academy for Eating Disorders (AED)
www.aedweb.org
Families Empowered and Supporting Treatment of Eating Disorders (F.E.A.S.T.)**
www.feast-ed.org
Eating Disorders Mentoring (EDM)
www.eatingdisordermentoring.org
International Association of Eating Disorder Professionals (IAEDP)
www.iaedp.com

Australia

Australia and New Zealand Academy for Eating Disorders
www.anzaed.org.au
The Butterfly Foundation
www.thebutterflyfoundation.org.au
   The Butterfly Foundation provides counselling support, information and referrals. Support Line calls are free in Australia: Dial 1800 ED HOPE (1800 33 4673) or email: support@thebutterflyfoundation.org.au. The Butterfly Foundation also provides contact details for locally based support groups and support organisations within Australia.

The National Eating Disorders Collaboration
www.nedc.com.au
    The National Eating Disorders Collaboration (NEDC) website provides young people and their families with access to clear, evidence-based, consistent information. The website includes an online directory of Australian specialist treatment services for eating disorders.

Canada

Bulimia Anorexia Nervosa Association
www.bana.ca
Danielle's Place (Burlington)
www.daniellesplace.org
Looking Glass Foundation**
www.lookingglassbc.com
NEDIC (National Eating Disorder Information Centre)
www.nedic.ca/

Ireland

Eating Disorder Resource Centre of Ireland
www.eatingdisorders.ie
ED Contact**
www.edcontact.com

New Zealand

Eating Disorders Association of New Zealand (EDANZ)**
www.ed.org.nz

United Kingdom

Anorexia and Bulimia Care
www.anorexiabulimiacare.org.uk
Anorexia Carers**
www.anorexiacarers.co.uk
Beat (Eating Disorders Association)
www.b-eat.co.uk
The New Maudsley Approach
http://thenewmaudsleyapproach.co.uk/FAQ.php

United States

A Chance to Heal**
http://achancetoheal.org

Alliance for Eating Disorders Awareness
www.allianceforeatingdisorders.com
Amy Helpenstell Foundation
amyhelpenstell.org/
Amy's Gift
www.trinityqc.com/Medical-Services/-Medical-Services-eatingdisorders.aspx
ANAD: National Association of Anorexia Nervosa and Associated Disorders
www.anad.org
Andrea's Voice**
www.andreasvoice.org
Anna Westin Foundation**
www.annawestinfoundation.org
Binge Eating Disorder Association (BEDA)
www.bedaonline.com/aboutus.html
Eating for Life Alliance
www.eatingforlife.org/
Gurze Books
www.bulimia.com
Hope Network**
http://hopenetwork.info
Maudsley Parents**
www.maudsleyparents.org
MentorConnect
www.key-to-life.com/mentorconnect
Multiservice Eating Disorders Association (MEDA)
www.medainc.org
The Elisa Project
www.theelisaproject.org/
The National Association for Males With Eating Disorders (NAMED)
www.namedinc.org
National Eating Disorders Association
www.nationaleatingdisorders.org
NEDA network members
www.nationaleatingdisorders.org/about-us/neda-network.php#members
Ophelia's Place, Inc.**
http://opheliasplace.org
Proud2bme – online community created for and by teens
http://proud2bme.org and http://www.proud2bme.nl/

Note: This list of organisations is largely sourced from: http://feast-ed.org/
LocalSupport/AdvocacyandSupportOrganizations.aspx

Resources

Knowledge will help you to confront and overcome an eating disorder. The book titles and web links provided here are a sample of the literature and support available to assist you in your journey.

Other titles by Janet Treasure and June Alexander

Alexander, June et al. (2013) *A Clinician's Guide to Binge Eating Disorder.* Abingdon: Routledge.

Alexander, June and Sangster, Cate (2013) *ED Says U Said – Eating Disorder Translator.* London: Jessica Kingsley Publishers.

Alexander, June (2011) *A Girl Called Tim – Escape from an Eating Disorder Hell.* Sydney: New Holland.

Alexander, June and Le Grange, Daniel (2010, 2011) *My Kid is Back – Empowering Parents to Beat Anorexia Nervosa.* Abingdon: Routledge.

Alexander, June and Treasure, Janet (2011) *A Collaborative Approach to Eating Disorders.* Abingdon: Routledge.

Treasure, Janet et al. (2007) *Skills-Based Learning for Caring for a Loved One with an Eating Disorder: The New Maudsley Method.* Abingdon: Routledge.

Schmidt, Ulrike, and Treasure, Janet (1993) *Getting Better Bit(e) by Bit(e).* Hove: Brunner-Routledge.

Treasure, Janet (1997) *Anorexia Nervosa: A Survival Guide for Sufferers and Those Caring for Someone with an Eating Disorder.* Hove: Psychology Press.

Anorexia nervosa – its effect on the brain

Arnold, Carrie (2012) *Decoding Anorexia – How Breakthroughs in Science Offer Hope for Eating Disorders.* Abingdon: Routledge.

Lask, Bryan and Frampton, Ian (2011) *Eating Disorders and the Brain.* Chichester: Wiley.

Parents

Brown, Harriet (2010) *Brave Girl Eating.* New York: William Morrow.

Collins, Laura (2004) *Eating with Your Anorexic: How My Child Recovered Through Family-Based Treatment and Yours Can Too.* New York: McGraw-Hill.

Henry, Becky (2011) *Just Tell Her to Stop: Family Stories of Eating Disorders.* Carol Stream, IL: Infinite Hope Publishing.

Education – schools

Atkinson, M. and Hornby, G. (2002) *Mental Health Handbook for Schools.* Abingdon: Routledge.

Capuzzi, D. and Gross, D.R. (2008) *Youth at Risk: A Prevention Resource for Counselors, Teachers, and Parents.* Alexandria, VA: American Counseling Association.

Cook-Cottone, C. (2009) Eating disorders in childhood: prevention and treatment supports. *Childhood Education*, 85, 5: 300.

Favaro, A., Zanetti, T., Huon, G. and Santonastaso, P. (2005) Engaging teachers in an eating disorder preventive intervention. *The International Journal of Eating Disorders*, 38, 1: 73–77.

Knightsmith, P. (2012) *Eating Disorders Pocketbook*. Hampshire: Teachers' Pocketbooks.

Prever, M. (2006) *Mental Health in Schools – A Guide to Pastoral and Curriculum Provision*. London: Paul Chapman Publishing.

Yager, Z. and O'Dea, J. (2010) A controlled intervention to promote a healthy body image, reduce eating disorder risk and prevent excessive exercise among trainee health education and physical education teachers. *Health Education Research*, 25, 5: 841–852.

www.eatingdisordersadvice.co.uk
This website provides eating disorders support and advice aimed at teachers.
www.eatingdisordersadvice.co.uk/policy/
This link provides a model eating disorders policy that can be adapted for use in your school.

Family-based treatment

Alexander, June and Le Grange, Daniel (2010, 2011) *My Kid is Back – Empowering Parents to Beat Anorexia Nervosa*. Abingdon: Routledge.

Le Grange, Daniel and Lock, James (2011) *Eating Disorders in Children and Adolescents: A Clinical Handbook*. New York: Guilford Press.

Le Grange, Daniel and Lock, James (2007) *Treating Bulimia in Adolescents: A Family-Based Approach*. New York: Guilford Press.

Lock, James and Le Grange, Daniel (2005) *Help Your Child Beat an Eating Disorder*. New York: Guilford Press.

Lock, James and Le Grange, Daniel (2012) *Treatment Manual for Anorexia Nervosa: A Family-Based Approach*, second edition. New York: Guilford Press.

Eating disorders in midlife

Bulik, Cynthia (2013) *Midlife Eating Disorders: Your Journey to Recovery*. London: Walker Publishing.

General

American Academy of Pediatrics. Committee on Adolescence (2003) Identifying and treating eating disorders. *Pediatrics*, 111, 1: 204–211.

Costin, C. (2007) *The Eating Disorder Sourcebook: A Comprehensive Guide to the Causes, Treatments, and Prevention of Eating Disorders*. New York: McGraw-Hill.

Cubic, B. (2002) Overcoming eating disorders: a cognitive-behavioral treatment for bulimia nervosa and binge-eating disorder: therapist guide patient workbook by W. Stewart Agra and Robin F. Apple. *Journal of Cognitive Psychotherapy*, 16: 250–251.

Golden, Neville H. and Meyer, Wendy (2003) *Nutritional Rehabilitation of Anorexia Nervosa. Goals and Dangers.* Online: www.sterlingnutrition.com/images/pdf/Nutrition Rehabilitation.pdf. (accessed 15 February 2013).

Lask, B. and Bryant-Waugh, R. (2007) *Eating Disorders in Childhood and Adolescence*. Abingdon: Routledge.

Mehler, P.S. and Andersen, A.E. (1999) *Eating Disorders: A Guide to Medical Care and Complications*. Baltimore: Johns Hopkins University Press.

Michel, D.M. and Willard, S.G. (2003) *When Dieting Becomes Dangerous: A Guide to Understanding and Treating Anorexia and Bulimia*. New Haven: Yale University Press.

Schwartz, Jeffrey with Beyette, Beverley (1996) *Brain Lock: Free Yourself from Obsessive-Compulsive Behaviour*. London: HarperCollins.

The anthropology of food and body: gender, meaning, and power. Reprinted from *Eating Disorders Review* (2000) 11, 1. Gürze Books (C.M. Counihan, Routledge, 1999).

WHO (1985) *World Health Organization Technical Report Series 724: Energy and Protein*. Geneva: WHO. Online: www.fao.org/docrep/003/AA040E/AA040E00.HTM (accessed 3 January 2013).

Williams, Pamela M., Goodie, Jeffrey and Motsinger, Charles D. (2008) *Treating Eating Disorders in Primary Care*. Online: www.aafp.org/afp/2008/0115/p187.html. (accessed 15 February 2013).

Stories of survival, regaining and restoring life

Alexander, June (2011) *A Girl Called Tim – Escape from an Eating Disorder Hell*. London: New Holland.

Cutts, Shannon (2009) *Beating Ana – How to Outsmart Your Eating Disorder and Take Your Life Back*. Deerfield Beach, FL: Health Communications Inc.

Liu, Aimee (2007) *Gaining – The Truth About Life After Eating Disorders*. New York: Warner Books.

Liu, Aimee (2011) *Restoring Our Bodies, Reclaiming Our Lives: Guidance and Reflections on Recovery from Eating Disorders*. London: Trumpeter Books.

Schaefer, Jenni with Rutledge, Thom (2003) *Life without Ed: How One Woman Declared Independence from Her Eating Disorder and How You Can Too*. Columbus, OH: McGraw-Hill.

Schaefer, Jenni (2009) *Goodbye Ed, Hello Me: Recover from Your Eating Disorder and Fall in Love with Life*. Columbus, OH: McGraw-Hill.

Thomas, Jennifer J. and Schaefer, Jenni (2013) *Almost Anorexic: Is My (or My Loved One's) Relationship with Food a Problem?* Center City, MN: Hazelden.

Dieting culture, body image, feminist texts

Bacon, Linda (2008) *Health at Every Size*. Dallas, TX: BenBella Books Inc.

Bulik, Cynthia (2009) *Crave – Why You Binge and How to Stop*. London: Walker Publishing.

Bulik, Cynthia (2011) *Woman in the Mirror – How to Stop Confusing What You Look Like with Who You Are*. London: Walker Publishing.

Cooper, M.J., Deepaky, K., Grocutty, E. and Bailey, E. (2007) The experience of 'feeling fat' in women with anorexia nervosa, dieting and non-dieting women: an exploratory study. *European Easting Disorders Review*, 15: 366–372.

Forbush, K., Heatherton, T. and Keel, P. (2007) Relationships between perfectionism and specific disordered eating behaviors. *International Journal of Eating Disorders*, 40: 37–41.

Frankel, Ellen and Matz, Judith (2004) *Beyond A Shadow of A Diet – The Therapist's Guide to Treating Compulsive Eating*. Hove: Brunner-Routledge.

Frazer, Ron (2006) *Anorexia Nervosa, Societal Causes, and Solutions*. Online: www. psychologytoday.com/blog/hunger-artist/201011/starvation-study-shows-recovery- anorexia-is-possible-only-regaining-weight (accessed 3 January 2013).

Gaesser, Glen (2002) *Big Fat Lies – The Truth About Your Weight and Health*. Carlsbad, CA: Gurze Books.

Hayaki, J., Friedman, M.A., Whisman, M.A., Delinsky, S.S. and Brownell, K.D. (2003) Sociotropy and bulimic symptoms in clinical and nonclinical samples. *International Journal of Eating Disorders*, 34: 172–176.

Katrina, Karin, King, Nancy and Hayes, Dayle (2003) *Moving Away from Diets – Healing Eating Problems and Exercise Resistance*. London: Helm Publishing.

Kilbourne, Jean (1999) *Can't Buy My Love*. New York: Touchstone.

Lelwica, Michelle (2010) *The Religion of Thinness*. Carlsbad, CA: Gurze Books.

Matz, Judith and Frankel, Ellen (2006) *The Diet Survivor's Handbook*. Naperville, IL: Sourcebooks.

Michel, Deborah Marcontell and Willard, Susan G. (2003) *When Dieting Becomes Dangerous*. New Haven: Yale University Press.

Neumark-Sztainer, Dianne (2005) *I'm, Like, SO Fat*. New York: Guildford Press.

Nilsson, K., Sundbom, E. and Hagglof, B. (2008) A longitudinal study of perfectionism in adolescent onset anorexia nervosa-restricting type. *European Eating Disorders Review*, 16: 386–394.

Ojeda, Linda (2008) *Safe Dieting for Teens*. London: Sheldon Press.

Roth, Geneen (2011) *Women, Food & God: An Unexpected Path to Almost Everything*. New York: Scribner.

Sansone, R.A. and Sansone, L.A. (2011). Personality pathology and its influence on eating disorders. *Clinical Neuroscience*, 8: 14–18.

Strober, M. and Johnson, C. (2012).The need for complex ideas in anorexia nervosa: why biology, environment, and psyche all matter, why therapists make mistakes, and why clinical benchmarks are needed for managing weight correction. *International Journal on Eating Disorders*, 5, 2:155–178.

Turner, J. M., Bulsara, M.K., McDermott, B.M., Byrne, G.C., Prince, R.L. and Forbes, D.A. (2000) Predictors of low bone density in adolescent females with anorexia nervosa and other dieting disorders. *International Journal of Eating Disorders*, 30: 245–251.

Professional

Malson, Helen and Burns, Maree (2009) *Critical Feminist Approaches to Eating Disorders*. Abingdon: Routledge.

Disordered eating

Ross, Carolyn (2009) *The Binge Eating and Compulsive Overeating Workbook: An Integrated Approach to Overcoming Disordered Eating*. Oakland, CA: New Harbinger Publications.

Feeding children

Satter, Ellyn (2005) *Your Child's Weight: Helping without Harming*. Madison, WI: Kelcy Press.

Recovery

Birgegard, A., Bjorck, C., Norring, C. Sholberg, S. and Clinton, D (2009) Anorexic self-control and bulimic self-hate: differential outcome prediction from initial self-image. *International Journal of Eating Disorders*, 46, 6: 522–530.

Cabrera, Dena and Wierenga, Emily (2013) *Mom in the Mirror: Body Image, Beauty, and Life After Pregnancy*. Lanham, MD: Rowman and Littlefield.

Costin, Carolyn and Schubert Grabb, Gwen (2011) *8 Keys to Recovery from an Eating Disorder: Effective Strategies from Therapeutic Practice and Personal Experience*. London: W.W. Norton and Company.

Couturier, J. and Lock, J. (2006) What is recovery in adolescent anorexia nervosa? *International Journal of Eating Disorders*, 39: 212–216.

Johnston, Anita (2000) *Eating in the Light of the Moon: How Women Can Transform Their Relationships with Food Through Myths, Metaphors and Storytelling*. Carlsbad, CA: Gurze Books.

Maine, Margo with Kelly, Joe (2005) *The Body Myth: Adult Women and the Pressure to Be Perfect*. Chichester: John Wiley.

Noordenbos, G. (2011). When have eating disordered patients recovered and what do the DSM-IV criteria tell about recovery? *Eating Disorders*, 19: 234–245.

Parker, Julie (2012) *My Recovery: Inspiring Stories, Recovery Tips and Messages of Hope from Eating Disorder Survivors*. Momentum Books.

Siegel Michele, Brisman Judith and Weinshel, Margot (2009) *Surviving an Eating Disorder: Strategies for Family and Friends*. Bloomington, IN: First Collins Living.

Tribole, Evelyn and Resch, Elyse (2012) *Intuitive Eating*, third edition. New York: St Martin's Griffin.

Weight stigma

Puhl, Rebecca, Rudd Center, Yale. *Weight Bias and Stigma*. Online: www.yaleruddcenter.org/what_we_do.aspx?id=10 (accessed 15 February 2013).

History

Bruch, H. (1982). *Anorexia Nervosa: Therapy and Theory*. New York: American Psychiatric Association.

Brumberg, Joan Jacobs (2000) *Fasting Girls: The History of Anorexia Nervosa*. New York: Vintage Books.

Gordon, Richard A. (2000) *Eating Disorders: Anatomy of a Social Epidemic*, second edition. Malden, MA: Blackwell Publishers.

Gull, W.W. (1868). The address in medicine. Delivered before the annual meeting of the British Medical Association at Oxford. *Lancet,* 2:171–176.

Gull, W.W. (1874) Anorexia nervosa (apepsia hysterica, anorexia hysterica). *Transactions of the Clinical Society of London*, 7: 22–28.

Janet, P. (1903) *The Major Symptoms of Hysteria*. London: Macmillan.

Lasegue, E.C. (1873) De l'anorexie hysterique. *Archives Generale de Medecine*, 21: 385–403.

Marce, L.V. (1860) On a form of hypochondriachal delirium occurring consecutive to dyspepsia and characterised by refusal offood. *Journal of Psychological Medicine and Mental Pathology*, 13: 264–266.

Morton, R. (1694) *Phthisiologia, or a Treatise of Consumptions*. London: Smith and Walford.

Reynolds, J. (1669). 'A discourse on prodigious abstinence' quoted in J.A. Silverman (1986) Anorexia nervosa in seventeenth-century England as viewed by physician, philosopher and pedagogue. *International Journal of Eating Disorders*, 5: 847–853.

Ryle, J.A. (1936). Anorexia nervosa. *Lancet*, ii: 893–899.

Effects of starvation

Keys, A., Brozeck, J., Henschel, A., Michelson, O. and Taylor, H. (1950) *The Biology of Human Starvation*. Minneapolis, MN: University of Minnesota Press.

Schocken, D.D., Holloway, J.D. and Powers, P.S. (1989) Weight loss and the heart. Effects of anorexia nervosa and starvation. *Arch Intern Med.*, 149, 4: 877–881.

Solzhenitsyn, Alexander (1962) *One Day in the Life of Ivan Denisovich*. New York: New American Library.

Troscianko, Emily T. (2010) *A Hunger Artist* – Starvation study shows that recovery from anorexia is possible only by regaining weight: Anorexia is a physical illness of starvation. Online: www.psychologytoday.com/blog/hunger-artist/201011/starvation-study-shows-recovery-anorexia-is-possible-only-regaining-weight (accessed 3 January 2013).

Tucker, Todd (2006) *The Great Starvation Experiment: The Heroic Men Who Starved so That Millions Could Live*. New York: Free Press.

Vonnegut, Kurt (1992) *Slaughterhouse-Five – A Novel*. New York: Dell Publishing.

Irvin Lucy (1984) *Castaway*. London: Penguin.

Culture

Chang, Jung (1991) *Wild Swans*. London: HarperCollins.

Websites for support and information

- www.eatingresearch.com
  The eating disorders research team based at the Institute of Psychiatry in south London has developed this website. The team works to find out more about the causes of anorexia nervosa, bulimia nervosa and other eating disorders, and to develop new and better treatments and ways of supporting carers.
- www.thenewmaudsleyapproach.co.uk
  This new website development contains tools for families and for professionals working with families.
- www.feast-ed.org
  Families Empowered And Supporting Treatment of Eating Disorders – F.E.A.S.T. is an international organisation of and for parents and caregivers to help loved ones recover from eating disorders by providing information and mutual support, promoting evidence-based treatment, and advocating for research and education to reduce the suffering associated with eating disorders.

- www.aroundthedinnertable.org
  This is a forum among peers for parents and carers of eating disorder patients.
- www.b-eat.co.uk
  Beat is the leading UK-wide charity providing information, help and support for people affected by eating disorders.
- http://www.yogaforcarers.com/index.html
  Carers who want to relax but don't know how – this site is for you.
- www.edbites.com
  ED BITES, by Carrie Arnold, provides the latest tasty tidbits in eating disorder science.

Videos

You may find the following cartoons helpful. They have been especially made for Professor Treasure and her research team to illustrate eating disorder scenarios and responses:

- www.youtube.com/user/EatingResearch
- www.youtube.com/user/CandMedProductions

Further reading

Gürze Books has specialised in eating disorders publications and education since 1980: www.bulimia.com/patient/patient_pages/eating_disorders_categories.cfm.

Appendix: tracking recovery

Sufficient food is crucial to recovery from an eating disorder. The following table provides estimates of calorie requirements to get you on your way.

What do I need to eat?

Your resting energy expenditure is 1500–2000 calories and then, if you are up and about, there is extra energy expenditure. Table App. 1 shows the metabolic rate for each body organ. The more active each organ is, the more energy is needed. This produces your daily energy expenditure. (DEE)

Table App. 1 Metabolic rate for body organs

Organ	Specific metabolic rate kcal/kg/day
Heart	440
Kidney	440
Brain	240
Liver	200
Skeletal Muscle	13
Rest	12

To gain weight

In order to gain weight you need additional calories. Every 1kg of weight gain needs about 7000 calories. So, to gain 1kg in a week, you will need to eat your DEE plus 1000 calories every day.

Most people aim to gain about 0.5 kg per week, so need to eat their DEE plus 500 calories per day.

Make your own weight gain plan. Below is an example.

- I want to gain _____ kg per week
- To do this I need to eat _____ (DEE calories) + _____ (extra calories per day)
- Therefore, I need to aim to eat a total of _____ calories per day.

How to plan meals

Most people find it helpful if the calorie intake is spread so that they are eating small amounts often throughout the day. Aim for foods that give a slow steady increase in energy (foods with a low glycaemic index) rather than highly processed, palatable foods that produce rapid energy fluxes.

What do the results from my examination mean?

Table App. 2 is a guide to some of the things that measure your physical health and that contribute to risk. Your doctor also will use a more global physical review and examination.

Table App. 2 Physical health risk measurements

System	Examination	High Risk	Severe Risk
Nutrition	BMI	<15	<13
	Weight loss or gain/wk	>0.5kg	>1.0kg
Circulation	Systolic Blood Pressure	<90	<80
	Diastolic Blood Pressure	<70	<60
	Pulse rate	<50	<40
	Extremities		Dark blue/white/ cold
Musculo – skeletal	Weakness lifting arms and legs	+	++
Temperature	<35	<34.5	
Investigations	Bone marrow	Concern if outside normal limits	
	Blood salts: sodium, potassium, phospate etc		
	Liver		
	Kidney		
	Blood sugar		

Steps forward and the recovery ruler

Most people find that the process of recovery involves taking small steps forward and keeping the bigger picture of a full life in mind in the face of dips in determination and motivation. Nine months is an estimate of recovery time – this can vary widely, depending on many factors.

Choose your goal wisely. Not too big or you will fail, nor too small so that you do not get a warm glow of a challenge met.

Set SMART goals, that is, goals that are:

- Specific
- Measurable
- Achievable
- Realistic
- Timely.

Recovery ruler

The recovery ruler is a useful tool when deciding how to implement goals.
  Ask yourself the following questions:

- How important is it for you to meet the goal?
- What are your desires, reasons and needs for reaching the goal?
- What score would you give yourself out of ten on your readiness to reach the goal?

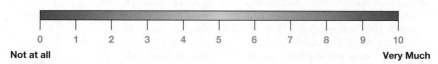

| 0 1 2 3 4 5 6 7 8 9 10 |
| **Not at all**   **Very Much** |

When you have done this, reflect on the following questions:

- Why have you given yourself this score, rather than 0 or 10?
- What could enable you to have a higher score?
- What would you notice about yourself if you had a higher score?
- What resources would you have to draw on to get to a higher score?
- Would other people be able to help you get to a higher score?
- What might others do to help you get to a higher score?
- What strategies have you used in the past that may help you get to a higher score?

Keep track of your recovery project:

- Keep a journal to track goal work
- Reflect regularly with your recovery guide. What have you learned? What is your next step?

Index